When I read my first J[e]
I had the sense that eve
prayed over, and carefully prepared. Each ensuing book
me to the same conclusion. The writings of Jerry Bridges are
a gift to the church. In this new book, he addresses a relevant
topic with the wisdom of a scholar and the heart of a servant.

MAX LUCADO
Pastor and bestselling author

Jerry Bridges helps us remember that the starting point of
true humility is a deep understanding of who God is. The
more we know Him, the more we can know our true selves.
This exploration of humility is humbling—because it will help
you see God more clearly.

KYLE IDLEMAN
Bestselling author and pastor, Southeast Christian Church

The Blessing of Humility gives us Jerry Bridges at his best: a
lifetime of prayer and meditation on Jesus' first and definitive
sermon that frames a life lived in the Kingdom of God under
conditions exclusively characterized (eight times!) by blessings.

EUGENE PETERSON
Professor Emeritus of Spiritual Theology, Regent College, Vancouver, B.C.

For many, the Beatitudes are beautiful but remote. They
hold poetic images but don't really seem relevant for life.
Throughout this wonderful book, Jerry Bridges shows us the
grace that's found when we walk humbly with Christ and
the joy that comes from resting in His finished work on the
cross. Finally, someone humble wrote a book on humility.

C.J. MAHANEY
Author of *Humility* and *True Greatness*

Jerry Bridges masterfully helps us not just understand but also
enter into living out the countercultural Beatitudes of Jesus.

Jerry does this by removing the idea that it cannot be done, by dispelling the myths associated with how it might be done, and most of all by reminding us that when it is done, it's done through the work of God's Spirit in our lives. It's not just a message on humility; it speaks of a person who is humbly living out the message that he has put to paper.

TOM HUGHES
Lead pastor of Christian Assembly, Los Angeles, and author of *Curious*

I love Bridges's concept of "dependent responsibility." Throughout the book, he shows that there are things we must do. It is our responsibility, for example, to walk in humility. But we must depend on the work and power of the Holy Spirit. As we grow, we become more aware that it is always Him.

RICHARD DOSTER
Editor, *byFaith* magazine

Pride is not only a problem for the chest-pounding athlete but for the "gentle" Christian who views the people of the world as his enemies. For most of us, the cancer of pride remains hidden and undetected. Like a skilled physician, Jerry Bridges uses God's Word to expose it. Yet, also like a skilled physician, Jerry not only exposes the disease but also applies the balm of the gospel to promote healing and genuine spiritual growth. This book is for everyone who doesn't think he needs it.

MARK BATES
Senior pastor, Village Seven Presbyterian Church, Colorado Springs

This is a Bible-saturated, theologically precise, and gospel-framed devotional book for those seeking more of Jesus and less of self in their lives.

FELIPE ASSIS
Senior pastor, Crossbridge Miami

the

BLESSING

of

HUMILITY

JERRY BRIDGES

A NavPress resource published in alliance
with Tyndale House Publishers, Inc.

NavPress is the publishing ministry of The Navigators, an international Christian organization and leader in personal spiritual development. NavPress is committed to helping people grow spiritually and enjoy lives of meaning and hope through personal and group resources that are biblically rooted, culturally relevant, and highly practical.

For more information, visit www.NavPress.com.

Library of Congress Cataloging-in-Publication Data

Names: Bridges, Jerry, author.
Title: The blessing of humility : walk within your calling / Jerry Bridges.
Description: Colorado Springs : NavPress, 2016. | Includes bibliographical references.
Identifiers: LCCN 2016003093| ISBN 9781631466236 | ISBN 9781631466243 (e-pub)
| ISBN 9781631466250 (kindle)
Subjects: LCSH: Humility—Religious aspects—Christianity. | Humility—Biblical teaching.
| Beatitudes.
Classification: LCC BV4647.H8 B75 2016 | DDC 241/.4--dc23 LC record available at
http://lccn.loc.gov/2016003093

Printed in the United States of America

22   21   20   19   18   17   16
7   6   5   4   3

To our Lord Jesus Christ
Who expressed the ultimate act of humility
By shedding His blood on the cross for our sins.
Then I heard the voice of myriads of angels
Saying with a loud voice,
"Worthy is the Lamb who was slain,
to receive power and wealth and wisdom and might
and honor and glory and blessing!"

REVELATION 5:12

CONTENTS

A NOTE TO THE READER

This book can be read completely in about two hours or less. You may want to do that to get an overview of the book

However, the real value of this book will come as you then read each chapter reflectively and prayerfully. Ask God to help you see yourself as you really are in the light of each of the character traits covered in the eight Beatitudes. And then ask God to help you grow in the areas where you see yourself to be most needy.

INTRODUCTION

The character trait of humility is the second-most frequently taught trait in the New Testament, second only to love. At one time I counted fifty instances of love taught, either by precept or example, in the New Testament; I counted forty instances of humility. I regard these two traits as the foundational stones of Christian character. All other character traits, in one way or another, are built upon love and humility.

Yet we so seldom hear any message or read any books on these two subjects. I think this is because they are so intimidating to us. Any honest Bible teacher, whether in speaking or in writing, realizes how far short he or she comes to exemplifying either of these character traits, so there is a reluctance to teach on a subject where one has made so little progress. For years I was hesitant to teach on 1 Corinthians 13, the great love chapter, and I felt an even greater hesitancy to write on humility, lest I appear to be saying, "I am a humble person."

I eventually learned that the job of Bible teachers is to point to Scripture, not to ourselves. We can do this with love because we can point to 1 Corinthians 13 and say, "This is what love looks like in everyday life." But until recently I could never point to a single passage of Scripture and say, "This is what humility looks like."

Then a request to write a short article on the Beatitudes caused me to study them really for the first time. As I did so, I thought, *These expressions of Christian character are a description of humility in action.* At last, I thought, here is an objective description outside of myself that I can point to and say, "That's what humility looks like. That is humility in action in everyday life."

Of course 1 Corinthians 13 is not an exhaustive treatment of love. And the Beatitudes are not an exhaustive treatment of humility. But both give us a good place to start. And the truth is, none of us will ever attain perfection in the traits that are mentioned. So keep in mind that I am not saying, "This is who I am" but rather "This is who I would like to be, and I am praying that I will grow in these traits, even as I pray you will also." So let's work on them together.

As we study these traits in the Beatitudes, we need to keep in mind several truths:

First, all Christians are meant to display these characteristics. They reflect qualities of a normal Christian life. They are for the plumber as well as the preacher, for the manager in business as well as the missionary on the mission field. No one is so high in social or economic status in this world, or so gifted in ministry, that these Beatitudes do not apply to him or her. Rather they are meant to be seen in the life of every Christian, without exception.

Furthermore, these characteristics are not meant to be reflective of our personalities, or temperaments, or even spiritual giftedness. Some people are naturally more self-effacing than others; some Christians have the gift of mercy and others do not. But none of the traits demonstrated in the Beatitudes are about personality or temperament or spiritual gifts. They are what Paul, in Galatians 5:22-23, calls the fruit of the Spirit: the results of His work in our lives.

Third, our progress in growth in these traits does not determine our acceptance with God, either in our eternal salvation or in our day-to-day standing with Him. It is Christ's righteousness, not our own, that makes us acceptable to God day after day (more about this in chapter 10). I can guarantee you that if you are honest with yourself and you let the Beatitudes search you, you will see yourself to be a greater sinner than you thought yourself to be. And when that happens you must flee to the righteousness of Christ to keep from becoming discouraged.

The fourth truth is that we are dependent on the Holy Spirit for any progress we make. We are dependent on Him to work in us, and we are dependent on Him to enable us to work because His work makes possible our work (more on this in chapter 10).

So in dependence on the righteousness of Christ and the enabling power of the Holy Spirit, let's be "doers of the word, and not hearers only" (James 1:22).

1. Let's hide or "store up" these words in our hearts (see Psalm 119:11).
2. Let's pray over these traits, asking God to show us our deficiencies and to cause us to grow in them (see Psalm 119:33-37).

ACKNOWLEDGMENTS

In all my books I am indebted to various people who participate in one way or another.

Eric Lindsay, a friend from North Ireland, gave me a copy of *The Beatitudes for Today* by John Blanchard, which proved very helpful in writing this book.

Connie Trautman, my part-time administrative assistant, patiently typed on the computer my often hard-to-read handwriting and then retyped my numerous changes.

Bob Bevington wrote the discussion questions.

Don Simpson, my former editor (now retired), looked over the entire manuscript and made helpful suggestions.

Brian Teal and Rev. Bill Vogler offered helpful suggestions on one difficult chapter.

Don Pape, NavPress publisher, was continually supportive.

David Zimmerman, NavPress editor, makes me look like a better writer than I am.

Finally, I am grateful to my wife, Jane, who (although she had no direct part in the book) works hard to "keep the home fires burning" so that I may give myself to teaching and writing.

CHAPTER ONE

PRECEPTS AND PROMISES

*I therefore, a prisoner for the Lord, urge
you to walk in a manner worthy of the
calling to which you have been called, with
all humility and gentleness, with patience,
bearing with one another in love.*

EPHESIANS 4:1-2

I still vividly remember a statement I heard at a Bible study in January 1952. It literally changed my life. The essence of the statement was, "The Bible is meant to be applied in your everyday life." As obvious as that is to me today, it was a brand-new thought that night. I had grown up in church and had never strayed beyond its moral boundaries, but as far as I can remember, the application of Scripture to one's daily life had never been taught in our church.

But that night, upon hearing that statement, it was as if someone had turned on a light in my mind. I was a young officer in the navy at that time, so on my way back to my ship, I prayed, "God, starting tonight, would you help me to apply the Bible to my everyday life?"

"Everyday life" is the crucial part of that life-changing statement. In Ephesians 4:1, Paul urges us to "walk in a manner

1

worthy of the calling to which you have been called." In that context *walk* means to live out one's ordinary daily life, whether it's working at your job, doing the laundry, grocery shopping, or a myriad of other things we do in the course of an ordinary day.

As Paul expands on the meaning of a worthy walk, the first thing he mentions is humility. Think of what that means: As I drive down the street, as I interact with my spouse or my children, or with my coworkers at a job, or with the clerk at the grocery store, I am to do all of it with humility.

In the Greco-Roman world of Paul's day, humility was a despised trait. They viewed it as a sign of weakness. And our culture today is no different from that world of two thousand years ago. Maybe it's a little different in our Christian circles. We may even admire humility in someone else, but we have little desire to practice it ourselves.

But when Paul wrote, "walk . . . with all humility," he was not just speaking for himself; rather he was speaking as God's spokesman. The Bible is not an ordinary book reflecting the thoughts of the various writers. Rather, as Paul wrote in 2 Timothy 3:16, "All Scripture is breathed out by God." Peter helps us understand what that means when he wrote in 2 Peter 1:21, "Men spoke from God as they were carried along by the Holy Spirit." To be "carried along" means that the writers of Scripture were so guided by the Holy Spirit that they wrote exactly what He wanted them to write. That is why we frequently read in the Bible an expression such as "the Holy Spirit spoke beforehand by the mouth of David" (Acts 1:16). God "breathed out" His words through David (or other writers). So we can confidently say, "What the Bible says, God says," even though He says it through the mouth or pen of human beings.

The issue here is one of authority, and one meaning of authority is the right to command. Paul does not have the right to command us to walk in humility, but God does. And though, speaking to his friends (and to us today), Paul uses a softer word (*urge*), he is still conveying the idea that a life of humility is not an option for a believer to choose or reject. It is a command of God.

This is a crucial point, because in our frenetic world of today, such softer character traits as humility, gentleness, and patience often get ignored or even regarded as unreal expectations in the hustle and bustle of life. But if we want to apply the Bible's teaching to our daily lives, we cannot ignore the call to live our ordinary lives in a spirit of humility.

Ephesians 4:1-2 is not the only Scripture in which Paul urges us to practice humility. In Philippians 2:3 he writes, "Do nothing from selfish ambition or conceit, but in humility count others more significant than yourselves." And again in Colossians 3:12, he tells us to "put on . . . humility." Peter adds his voice in 1 Peter 5:5: "Clothe yourselves, all of you, with humility toward one another." These are not offhand statements made in passing. They are all the very words of God and carry with them the implied authority of God to command us to pursue humility in our everyday lives.

In addition to Paul and Peter, Jesus frequently addressed the subject of humility. Though He seldom used the word, the concept is scattered throughout His teaching. In fact the character traits in the Beatitudes, which constitute the major portion of this book, are all expressions of what I call "humility in action."

One of my favorite teachings of Jesus on humility is Luke 14:7-11, which I learned many years ago. I *try* (note the emphasis) to practice the principle He taught on appropriate occasions.

> *Now he told a parable to those who were invited, when he noticed how they chose the places of honor, saying to them, "When you are invited by someone to a wedding feast, do not sit down in a place of honor, lest someone more distinguished than you be invited by him, and he who invited you both will come and say to you, 'Give your place to this person,' and then you will begin with shame to take the lowest place. But when you are invited, go and sit in the lowest place, so that when your host comes he may say to you, 'Friend, move up higher.' Then you will be honored in the presence of all who sit at table with you. For <u>everyone who exalts himself will be humbled, and he who humbles himself will be exalted.</u>"*

LUKE 14:7-11

To apply Jesus' teaching to our present-day culture, we need to think in terms not of a seat of honor but of positions, of prestige, recognition, or authority, which most of us are tempted to seek after. Instead, a good rule to follow is found in the words of Proverbs 27:2: "<u>Let another praise you, and not your own mouth; a stranger, and not your own lips.</u>"

Jesus not only taught humility; He practiced it Himself. We see this in His washing of the disciples' feet at the Last Supper (see John 13:1-11). What makes His act even more striking is that He did this in full awareness that He was the eternal Son of God (verse 3). And we see His ultimate humility, as He humbled Himself even to death on the cross for our sake (Philippians 2:8).

I've titled this chapter "Precepts and Promises," but so far I've used neither word in the text of the chapter. A precept, however, is a synonym for a command. In fact, my dictionary defines *precept* as "an order [or command] issued by a legally constituted authority." And of course there's no greater authority than God. A *promise*, meanwhile, is a declaration that gives a person the right to expect the performance of that which is promised. Only God has the infinite power and absolute integrity to fulfill that which He has promised.

So now let's move to God's promises to those who walk in humility. The apostle Peter joins precept and promise together in 1 Peter 5:5-6:

> *Clothe yourselves, all of you, with humility toward one another, for "God opposes the proud but gives grace to the humble."*
>
> *Humble yourselves, therefore, under the mighty hand of God so that at the proper time he may exalt you.*

In verse 5 the precept is "clothe yourselves . . . with humility." That is, humility should be as much a part of us as the clothes we wear. We wouldn't think of appearing before other people without our clothes. And we shouldn't think of appearing before other people without deliberately clothing ourselves with an attitude of humility.

The promise is that God gives grace to the humble. *Grace* is often used as a synonym for God's power (see, for example, 2 Timothy 2:1; 2 Corinthians 12:9), and that is its meaning here. An attitude of humility is completely contrary to the world's values, but also contrary to our own sinful nature. So we need God's grace—that is, His Spirit-supplied enablement—to clothe ourselves with an attitude of humility as we encounter different people and different situations throughout the day. And God promises us He will supply that grace, as we seek to walk in humility.

While verse 5 speaks of humility with regard to other people, verse 6 speaks of humility toward God: "Humble yourselves, therefore, under the mighty hand of God so that at the proper time he may exalt you." To humble oneself under the mighty hand of God is to submit to and accept even adverse providential circumstances from God (more about this in chapter 4).

The promise of verse 6 is that at the proper time God will exalt you. What that exaltation will look like, and the proper time of it, is left undetermined because it can come in many ways and at various times. Only God knows the proper time and expression of His exaltation. And it may not come in this life, but it will come because God, who cannot lie, has promised it.

Now let's look at two Old Testament promises to those who seek to walk in humility. The first is Isaiah 57:15:

> For thus says the One who is high and lifted up,
>   who inhabits eternity, whose name is Holy:
> "I dwell in the high and holy place,
>   and also with him who is of a contrite and lowly spirit,
> to revive the spirit of the lowly,
>   and to revive the heart of the contrite."

As we consider this Scripture, first notice God's description of Himself. He is high and lifted up, and His name is holy. This passage is a reflection of Isaiah 6:1-7, in which Isaiah in a vision sees God as high and lifted up (that is, as exalted) and hears the seraphim cry out, "Holy, holy, holy is the LORD of hosts." As a result of seeing God in His magnificent glory, Isaiah was totally devastated. But in Isaiah 57:15 this same infinitely holy and exalted One promises to dwell with those who are of a contrite and lowly (that is, humble) spirit, and to revive their hearts.

In this context, to dwell with someone is to enter into an intimate relationship with that person. And to *revive* here means to encourage the person. This is a fantastic promise to go along with the precept to live a life of humility. Walking in humility will sometimes involve a sense of shame or even humiliation. As we humbly accept those situations, God promises to dwell with us and encourage us.

The second promise is Isaiah 66:1-2:

> *Thus says the LORD:*
> *"Heaven is my throne,*
>   *and the earth is my footstool;*
> *what is the house that you would build for me,*
>   *and what is the place of my rest?*
> *All these things my hand has made,*
>   *and so all these things came to be,*
> *declares the LORD.*
> *But this is the one to whom I will look:*
>   *he who is humble and contrite in spirit*
>   *and trembles at my word."*

Once again, in verse 1 and at the beginning of verse 2, we see the infinite majesty of God. Heaven is His throne, and the earth is only His footstool. In fact, He made it all. Yet even though God is infinite in His power and glory, there are those to whom He will look with affection and favor: those who are humble and contrite in spirit, and those who tremble (in profound respect) at His word. What a promise!

Combining these two passages of Scripture together: God promises those who will walk humbly that He will enter into an intimate relationship with them, look with favor and affection toward them, and encourage them in their pursuit of humility. Instead of despising humility, as the Greco-Roman culture did and as our present culture still does, God exalts it and promises to bless those who pursue it.

Does this not cause us to realize that the pursuit of humility is not an incidental thing—something we seldom think about—but rather a character trait that we should give diligent attention to? The very fact that we are so casual about humility should in itself cause us to humble ourselves in the dust before such a glorious and gracious God.

To recap what we have seen in this chapter, the pursuit of humility in our daily walk comes under the precepts—that is, the authoritative commands—of God. And Psalm 119:4 says, "You have commanded your precepts to be kept diligently." Humility is not an optional add-on for the super-spiritual; it is for all believers to practice in our daily lives. Furthermore, God has promised to give grace to us as we seek humility.

But what does humility look like as we pursue it every day? In the following eight chapters we will see how humility expresses itself in the different circumstances and people we encounter as we live out our daily lives in a broken and sin-cursed world. Our guide will be Jesus Himself, who began His longest recorded sermon with a litany of countercultural blessings known to us as the Beatitudes. Taken together, they offer a portrait of humility in action, something which God commands and which God promises to bless.

CHAPTER TWO

POOR IN SPIRIT

Blessed are the poor in spirit,
for theirs is the kingdom of heaven.

MATTHEW 5:3

I grew up in poverty until I was about fourteen years old. Those were years of the "Great Depression," and many men were out of work. My father did have a job, but he worked fifty hours a week for about forty-two cents an hour. We lived in a small, four-room house of about four hundred square feet. There were neither closets nor cabinets. We did have indoor plumbing, but no hot water except what we heated on the kitchen stove. Many nights our supper consisted of pinto beans and corn bread. The only books in the house were my parents' two Bibles. We had no toys.

Yes, I grew up in poverty—but not the depth of poverty Jesus was talking about when he used the expression "poor in spirit."

The Greek word that Jesus used for "poor" is the word *ptochos.* It is used to describe not ordinary poverty but abject poverty. *Ptochos* is not like my parents struggling to make ends meet. Rather it describes a person who is completely destitute and helpless to do anything about it.

Abject poverty is illustrated by Lazarus in the well-known parable in Luke 16:19-31. Lazarus was described by Jesus as a "poor man." The fact that he was laid at the rich man's gate indicates he was a cripple, helpless to do anything about his plight. He desired to be fed with what fell from the rich man's table. Unlike my childhood, he had no pinto beans and corn bread. He had nothing. In fact, Jesus did not tell us whether or not he *received* that which fell from the rich man's table. He only said that Lazarus *desired* it.

This is a picture of abject poverty, but even this is not the kind of poverty Jesus was talking about when He said, "Blessed are the poor in spirit." As used here, *spirit* refers to one's inner being, our self-awareness. Specifically here it means how we evaluate ourselves with regard to our own spiritual condition. This abject poverty of spirit comes from our awareness of our own dreadfully sinful condition.

"Poor in spirit" is probably best illustrated by the tax collector in Jesus' parable of the Pharisee and the tax collector (Luke 18:9-14). Everything about the man displays his poverty of spirit. He stands far off—we might say today that he takes the very last seat in the church. He does not lift his eyes; he is ashamed of his sin. He beats his breast; he is in agony about his sinful condition. But it is his prayer that really captures his poverty of spirit: "God, be merciful to me, a sinner!"

First of all, note his use of the word *merciful*. To us today that is a very ordinary word. But the Greek word, *hilaskomai*, translated here as "merciful," presupposes the just and holy wrath of

God toward our sin. The tax collector's cry is a cry for deliverance from that wrath which he knows he deserves.

Furthermore, contrary to our English translations, the little word *a* does not appear in the original language. Literally the tax collector says, "God, be merciful to me, sinner" (or "the sinner"). Author John Blanchard observes that the tax collector

> did not think of himself as one sinner among many, but as if he were the only one. He was so overwhelmed with the sense of his sin, his moral bankruptcy and his spiritual destitution that, as far as he was concerned, anyone else's sin paled into insignificance by comparison.[1]

The tax collector was poor in spirit. We may think that he deserved to be poor in spirit. After all, he was a tax collector, considered by his own countrymen as a traitor, collecting taxes for the Roman government, and becoming rich in the process. But consider Isaiah the prophet, who was undoubtedly a righteous man. One day he had a vision of God in His infinite majesty and moral purity (Isaiah 6:1-5). Isaiah's response was, "Woe is me! For I am lost; for I am a man of unclean lips, and I dwell in the midst of a people of unclean lips; for my eyes have seen the King, the LORD of hosts!"

The word *unclean* which Isaiah used was the word lepers were required to use as they walked along the road, crying, "Unclean, unclean" (Leviticus 13:45). In effect Isaiah was calling himself a moral leper. He was utterly devastated by his own sinfulness as he saw himself in the presence of the infinitely holy God. Isaiah was also poor in spirit.

This poverty of spirit is not just for the unbeliever recognizing his need of salvation. In the Beatitudes Jesus is talking about the character traits of those already in the kingdom. And He says we should be poor in spirit. It should be the ongoing daily attitude of one who is growing spiritually.

Believers who are growing continue to see more sin in their lives. It is not that they are sinning more; rather they are becoming more aware of and more sensitive to the sin that has been there all along. It is not the flagrant sins of society around us, but rather such sins as our selfishness, our pride, our jealousy and envy, and above all, our judgmental spirit toward others. And it is the realization that even these sins, which seem so minor in our eyes, would bring us under the wrath of God, were it not for the atoning blood of Christ shed for us on the cross, that should cause us to be poor in spirit.

Toward the end of his life the apostle Paul wrote, "Christ Jesus came into the world to save sinners, of whom I am the foremost" (1 Timothy 1:15). Paul used the present tense to describe himself: He didn't say, "I was" or "I used to be" but "I am." For Paul, poverty of spirit was a continuous self-assessment.

The person who is poor in spirit recognizes that his or her best deeds are always mingled with the corruption of one's sinful nature, with impure (that is, mixed) motives, and with imperfect performance. This person recognizes that he or she never comes close to obeying the law of God as Jesus defined it in Matthew 22:37-39: to love God with all our being, and to love our neighbor as ourselves.

At the same time, those who genuinely see their spiritual poverty do not wallow in it and say, "Oh, what a miserable Christian I am." Instead they look to Christ and His Cross for cleansing from their sin. They love (or would love if they knew it) the picturesque words of an old hymn by William Cowper (1731–1800), "There Is a Fountain."

> *There is a fountain filled with blood*
> *Drawn from Immanuel's vein;*
> *And sinners plunged beneath that flood,*
> *Lose all their guilty stain.*

The second stanza should be even more meaningful to those who are poor in spirit.

> *The dying thief rejoiced to see*
> *That fountain in his day;*
> *And there may I, though vile as he,*
> *Wash all my sin away.*

Does that resonate with you at all? Do you see yourself as vile as the thief hanging on the cross? If so, you are in good company, for Jesus said to the thief, "Truly, I say to you, today you will be with me in Paradise" (Luke 23:43). And remember the tax collector praying in the temple, "God, be merciful to me, [the] sinner"? Jesus said of him, "This man went down to his house justified" (that is, counted as righteous by God— Luke 18:13-14). So the poor in spirit mourn over their sin, as we will see in the next chapter, but at the same time they rejoice in the forgiveness of their sin, and the righteousness they have in Christ.

Those who are poor in spirit also resonate with the first words of another old hymn, "The Solid Rock," written by Edward Mote (1797–1874): "My hope is built on nothing less than Jesus' blood and righteousness." They see Christ's blood and righteousness as their hope not only for eternity but for

God's favor each day. They groan over their sin and earnestly pursue holiness, but they do not *trust* in their holiness. Instead they say, "We are unworthy servants; we have only done what was our duty" (Luke 17:10).

Poverty of spirit has to do primarily with our increasing awareness of our ongoing struggle with sin and our frequent failures. But it also expresses itself in other ways that display humility in action. For example, instead of minimizing or disregarding their sin while maximizing the sins of others, the poor in spirit do just the opposite: They identify with the tax collector praying in the temple, who regarded himself as the only sinner. They identify with the apostle Paul as the foremost of sinners. Those who are poor in spirit look upon other believers as better than themselves. They are like the apostle Paul, who considered himself "the least of the apostles" (1 Corinthians 15:9) and in fact, "the very least of all the saints" (that is, all believers—Ephesians 3:8). And when looking at themselves, those who are poor in spirit freely acknowledge that all they are, and anything they have accomplished, is because of the grace of God at work in them (1 Corinthians 15:10).

People who are poor in spirit also see themselves as utterly dependent on God and His grace in their entire lives. They recognize that they are dependent on God even for "life and breath" (Acts 17:25). They freely acknowledge that any abilities, talents, spiritual gifts, and accomplishments are gifts from God. They identify with Paul's words in 1 Corinthians 4:7:

> *For who sees anything different in you? What do you have*
> *that you did not receive? If then you received it, why do you*
> *boast as if you did not receive it?*

So instead of boasting or seeking recognition for themselves, they, like the apostle Paul, boast only in the cross of the Lord Jesus Christ (see Galatians 6:14).

Those who are poor in spirit do not murmur or complain about adverse circumstances God allows or brings into their lives. Instead they acknowledge that there is still much sin remaining in them, and that God often uses adversity to expose sin and to grow them more and more into conformity to Christ. (See Romans 8:28-29 and Hebrews 12:10-11; I wrote more about this in chapter 4.)

The person who is poor in spirit has a deep, awe-filled reverence for God and His Word. He or she wonders why the Creator and Sustainer of the universe should condescend to look on a mere creature—and a still-sinful creature at that. Therefore, this person delights to worship and adore this One who is infinite in His being, power, and holiness and who yet numbers the hairs on our heads.

Does it seem as if I am exaggerating our lowly condition? I think not. After all, it was Jesus who chose to use the Greek word *ptochos* to describe our spiritual condition. Other words, not nearly so strong, could have been used. It was Jesus who gave us the story of the rich man and Lazarus, and the parable of the tax collector praying in the temple, to help us understand what it means to be poor in spirit.

We live in a culture that promotes self-esteem. And I am concerned that this attitude has permeated the body of Christ. We see ourselves as better than we are. We look at sinful society around us, and we can be like the Pharisee who prayed, "God, I thank you that I am not like other men" (Luke 18:11).

As we read over this description of what it means to be poor in spirit, many of us will confess, "No, I am not poor in spirit." But we should pray that we will become so. As we saw in chapter 1, we are commanded to pursue humility, and I am convinced that true humility begins with and grows out of being poor in spirit. It is when we face the sinful attitudes and practices that still entangle us, when we begin to realize how desperately far short we fall from being the people God intends us to be, that we can begin to express humility in action.

CHAPTER THREE

MOURN

Blessed are those who mourn,
for they shall be comforted.

MATTHEW 5:4

"Blessed are those who mourn" is the Beatitude I approach with the greatest sense of inadequacy. I have done so little mourning over sin myself. Regret, yes; sorrow, yes. Even tears on occasion. But Jesus was talking about very deep mourning over sin when He said, "Blessed are those who mourn."

As we approach this subject, we need to keep two truths in mind. First, these character traits are meant to be descriptive of all Christians. Second, none of us will ever exhibit any of these traits to the fullest. But we should all earnestly desire to grow in them. And one of the most difficult traits to grow in is mourning over our sin.

The word that Jesus used in this Beatitude is the strongest word in the Greek language for mourning. It is the word for Jacob's mourning over what he thought was the death of Joseph (Genesis 37:35). It is used again of those who were mourning and weeping over the death of Jesus (Mark 16:10). Jesus uses this word to show the intensity of mourning He blesses here. He is, however, actually talking about mourning not over death but over our sin.

Each of the eight Beatitudes addresses a specific attitude of the heart. In this one Jesus is addressing our attitude toward our personal sin. James makes a similar point:

> Cleanse your hands, you sinners, and purify your hearts, you double-minded. Be wretched and mourn and weep. Let your laughter be turned to mourning and your joy to gloom. Humble yourselves before the Lord, and he will exalt you.
> JAMES 4:8-10

In this Beatitude, mourning is not just a touch of sadness but deep heartfelt grief, accompanied by tears, over one's sin. Probably very few Christians today ever experience this kind of mourning over sin, but Jesus said that those who do shall be blessed.

This second character trait of the Beatitudes naturally follows the first. Those who are genuinely poor in spirit will mourn over their sin. As John Blanchard wrote, "To be 'poor in spirit' is to be convicted of one's sin, whereas to 'mourn' is to be contrite for it."[1]

David's prayer as recorded in Psalm 51 is an example of mourning over sin. But before we look at this prayer, let's review the occasion for it, as recorded in 2 Samuel 11:1–12:15.

King David committed two sins: first adultery, and then (essentially) murder to try to cover up his adultery. God sent the prophet Nathan to confront him, and in his skillful accusation of David, Nathan twice used the word *despised* (2 Samuel 12:7-11). First, David despised the Word of the Lord—that is, he despised the law of God (verse 9). In so doing, he also despised the *person* of God (verse 10).

Why is this true? Despising the law of God is not only an expression of rebellion. It is also a despising of His very character, since His law is a reflection of His character. This is true not only of such heinous sins as adultery and murder, but also of our more refined sins: pride, selfishness, gossip, and the like. So let us pray that God will indeed allow us to see our sin as rebellion against the rule of God—a despising of God's law and even of His character.

With this in mind, now note the following words from Psalm 51:1-5:

> Have mercy on me, O God,
>   according to your steadfast love;
> according to your abundant mercy
>   blot out my transgressions.
> Wash me thoroughly from my iniquity,
>   and cleanse me from my sin! . . .
> Against you, you only, have I sinned
>   and done what is evil in your sight,
> so that you may be justified in your words
>   and blameless in your judgment.
> Behold, I was brought forth in iniquity,
>   and in sin did my mother conceive me.

David acknowledged both his transgressions (actual sinful acts) and his iniquity (the evil heart from which his sins flowed). Then he acknowledged he was sinful from birth. He sinned because he was born a sinner.

But probably the most important statement in his prayer

is "Against you, you only, have I sinned." All sin is primarily against God and His law. We may wrong our neighbor, but it is God's law that we have broken. It is God's glory that we have sinned against. We will never see the seriousness of our sin and mourn over it until we see that it is against God.

Failure to see our sin as primarily against God is, I believe, the reason we experience so little heartfelt grief over it. We tend to view our sin first in terms of its effect on ourselves. Sin makes us feel guilty, and we don't like to feel guilty. Then we may see our sin in terms of its effect on the other person. For example, we may have damaged his or her reputation with our gossip or unkind words. But we would just like to forget it and move on.

We fail to see that our sin is primarily against God. It is His law that we have broken. It is His holiness that we have defiled. Because of this, God hates our sin; He cannot look upon it with indifference.

The Puritans had a redundant but still very meaningful expression. They spoke of "the sinfulness of sin." What is it that makes sin so sinful? It is the fact that it is against God. Until we grasp this in the depths of our hearts, we will never mourn over our sin. That is why David's confession, "Against you, you only, have I sinned," is so important.

Having dealt with the seriousness of his sin, David proceeds to the remedy for it.

The sacrifices of God are a broken spirit;
a broken and contrite heart, O God, you will not despise.
PSALM 51:17

As David admitted the seriousness of his sin, he was deeply broken and contrite. We may think he *should* have been repentant and contrite. After all, he committed adultery with Bathsheba and had her husband killed in battle. Compared to such heinous grievances, we think our more mundane sins can be adequately grieved at a more mundane level. But be it ever so small in our own eyes, when we sin we also break God's law. And Scripture says, "Whoever keeps the whole law but fails in one point has become accountable for all of it" (James 2:10). God's law is seamless, one complete whole. So when we break any of it, we break the whole law.

I recall a time when I strongly identified with David in Psalm 51. His statement that God will not despise a broken and contrite heart deeply ministered to me. It wasn't that I had committed some big sin, as we evaluate different sins. My sin was a wrong motive.

My wife and I were invited to minister in a country overseas. When I received the invitation, I thought, *That would be a fun place to go.* After consulting my wife, I immediately said yes. I wasn't thinking about how I would serve the ministry that invited me or the people of that country. I was thinking of us. I knew I would be busy speaking and teaching God's Word, of course, and as always I wanted to do a good job. But my motive for going was self-centered, not God-centered!

The trip turned out to be a ministry disaster. In more than two dozen speaking and teaching sessions, I never felt that I had the power of the Holy Spirit giving life to my words.

As I continued to pray about the difficult situation, it seemed as if God said, "Why are you here?" And I realized that my motive had been primarily for our pleasure, not the benefit of God's people.

As I began to realize how seriously I had sinned against God,

I became brokenhearted and contrite about it. And that is when Psalm 51:17 deeply ministered to me.

I would like to say that upon my repentance, God immediately turned things around. But He didn't. I struggled with every message and teaching session the entire trip. Through that experience God drilled into my heart the importance of God-centered motives.

I use this personal illustration to impress on our hearts the seriousness of all sin. In that incident I didn't *do* anything wrong. I simply acted from a self-centered motive. And God was displeased with that.

Jesus pronounced a blessing on those who mourn—those who are brokenhearted and contrite over their sin. Yet we see so little mourning over sin today. Why is that true? I believe it is because we do not see ourselves as sinners. We do not take seriously such sins as our pride, our selfishness, and our judgmental spirit toward others. We may not utter the words of the Pharisee, "God, I thank you that I am not like other men" (Luke 18:11), but deep down that is too often our heart attitude.

Is mourning over sin just for those first coming to Christ? No, Jesus' words are in the present active tense. We could literally translate them as "blessed are those who continue to mourn." He is pronouncing a blessing on those whose attitude toward their sin is characterized by mourning. One mark of a growing Christian, then, is a growing sense of his or her sin, and an attitude of mourning over it.

Now we need to see the *blessing* of mourning over sin. Jesus did say that those who mourn shall be comforted. How will they be comforted? I think it is the experience of God's forgiveness. It is the assurance that "where sin increased, grace abounded all the more" (Romans 5:20), that though our "sins are like scarlet, they shall be as white as snow" (Isaiah 1:18).

Note how David ends Psalm 51. He is confident that God will not despise a broken and contrite heart. This is not just David's opinion or hope. Remember, he is writing under the divine guidance of the Holy Spirit (see 2 Peter 1:21). Thus David is saying what the Holy Spirit prompted and directed him to say. Knowing that what the Bible says, God also says, I sometimes like to restate a verse with God as the speaker. In this case, I restate it as God saying, "A broken and contrite heart I will not despise." Think of that! What greater comfort can one who is mourning over his sin receive? God will not despise my broken and contrite heart.

As we saw earlier, Jesus used the same word for mourning as the Bible uses for mourning over the death of a loved one. Jesus did this to show the intensity with which we should mourn over our sin. But there is a profound difference between the two causes of mourning. In the case of death, there is no hope of ever seeing that loved one again in this life. Most often at the time of mourning, especially in the case of sudden and unexpected death, the hope for eternity is of little comfort. We miss the person now, and the thought of never seeing our deceased loved one again in this life is overwhelming. As a result, we mourn deeply.

Mourning over our sin is different. Unlike death, there is hope in the here and now. If we are repentant, we can take that sin to the Cross and experience immediate forgiveness. We can experience the truth that God will not count that sin against us; He will not despise a broken and contrite heart.

Because of this we can be honest with ourselves about our

sin. We do not need to minimize it or try to excuse ourselves. Instead we can see it for the vile and despicable act of rebellion against God that it really is.

Our problem, however, is that we do not recognize the sin that still remains in us. We do not recognize that failing to love God with all our being, and to love our neighbors as ourselves, would bring us under the curse of God apart from the work of Christ on our behalf (Galatians 3:10). We do not see the immense chasm that exists between the infinite holiness of God and our own righteousness on our very best days. In short, we do not see ourselves as sinners—saved sinners to be sure, but still practicing sinners in need of the forgiving grace of God every day.

So mourning over our sin is truly a display of humility in action. We cannot be proud and mourn over sin at the same time. We cannot be judgmental toward other believers, or even toward unbelievers, if we are truly contrite and brokenhearted over our own sin.

There is yet one more application from this Beatitude we need to make. The Greek word that Jesus used for *mourn* is used twice elsewhere for mourning over sin: 1 Corinthians 5:2 and James 4:9. James uses it in the context of our sin, but Paul uses it in the context of tolerating the sin of someone else. I think that in Paul's use there is a lesson for us to apply in today's culture.

There is no question that our nation is sinking more deeply into gross sins of violence, immorality, murder (especially of the unborn), flagrant dishonesty, and other kinds of vile sins. What should be our attitude toward these sins? We have three options: condone it, condemn it, or mourn over it. We certainly don't condone it, but I think most of us merely condemn it.

It is the third option we should pursue, and the attitude of Ezra at the time of the Jews' return from exile can be an example to us. Ezra was a godly man; he "had set his heart to study the Law of the LORD, and to do it and to teach his statutes and rules in Israel" (Ezra 7:10). Although a godly man himself, Ezra identified with the sins of the people and mourned over them. When he learned that the returned exiles had again begun to intermarry with the idolatrous people of the land, he tore his garments (a sign of deep mourning), and prayed:

> *O my God, I am ashamed and blush to lift my face to you, my God, for our iniquities have risen higher than our heads, and our guilt has mounted up to the heavens.*
>
> EZRA 9:6

Notice how Ezra identifies himself with the sins of the people: *our* iniquities, *our* guilt. I believe this is the attitude we should pursue in our day. It is so easy for us to stand apart from the culture and do no more than express self-righteous judgmentalism toward it. But those of us who grieve deeply over our own sin will not do this. Instead we will mourn over the sins and wickedness of our nation and will pray most urgently that, just as we want God to be merciful to us, so we want Him to be merciful to our nation as a whole. This will be another expression of humility in action.

CHAPTER FOUR

MEEK

Blessed are the meek,
for they shall inherit the earth.

MATTHEW 5:5

A friend of mine who is an entrepreneur was listening to a CD of a series of messages I had given on the Beatitudes. When he came to meekness, he told me, he skipped over it. He wasn't interested in being meek. Like most Americans, he thought of a meek person as someone who is timid, spineless, unassertive, and easily dominated or intimidated. Some readers will recognize these traits as exemplified in a cartoon character of bygone years, Caspar Milquetoast, who has been described as a man who speaks softly and gets hit with a big stick.

The word for *meek* that Jesus used is far different. Meekness is not being timid, spineless, unassertive, and easily dominated. It is not a natural niceness. In fact, it has nothing to do with one's personality or temperament. It is the work of the Holy Spirit within. Yet it is a character trait that can and should be cultivated in our lives.

The Greek word *praus* is usually translated as either "meek" or "gentle," depending on the context. For purposes of this study I use meekness as our response to the often hurtful actions of other people or to the adversities God brings into our lives. There is then a twofold expression of meekness: first toward God and then toward other people. Meekness toward God involves

- responsiveness to His Word
- submission to His providence

Responsiveness to God's Word. To be responsive to God's Word is to approach it as one who is "poor in spirit"—to recognize that there is still much unbelief and sin in one's heart that needs to be exposed, acknowledged, repented of, and dealt with. The meek person reads Jesus' words in Matthew 5:48—"You therefore must be perfect, as your heavenly Father is perfect"—and realizes that however much he or she appears to be a nice person, they have not come close to the perfect righteousness God requires, which is to be found only in the perfect righteousness of Jesus Christ.

As I reflect on our evangelical community to the extent I am aware of it, it seems we are more *knowers* of the Word than *doers* of the Word. We sit in church on Sunday and hear an inspiring or challenging message, and we agree with what we hear. We may even say we enjoyed the sermon. But once we leave the church, we forget about it. The same is true in principle with weekly Bible studies. We do some study at home, we come together and discuss what we have learned, but we do not take it home to reflect and pray over, or seek to apply what we learned in our daily lives.

We do not receive with meekness the "implanted" Word

of God (James 1:21). Instead we too often use the Scriptures not as a means of judging ourselves but as a means of judging others, especially those whose sins are more flagrant than ours. The meek person, in contrast, searches the Scriptures (or listens to it taught) not to judge others but to allow the Holy Spirit to judge him or her. In fact, the meek person earnestly desires the Spirit to use His Word to effect a deep change in his or her inner being.

So we see that these character traits of the Beatitudes build on one another. Only the person who is "poor in spirit," who recognizes his or her own remaining spiritual poverty, and who "mourns" over his or her sin will want to be responsive to God's Word as a means of dealing with sin and growing in Christlike character.

Submission to God's providence requires first that we understand the meaning of the term. Briefly, for purposes of this study, *providence* refers to God's sovereign rule over His entire creation, controlling, directing, and orchestrating all events and circumstances to accomplish His purposes. In support of that statement consider the following Scriptures:

> For the LORD of hosts has purposed,
>   and who will annul it?
> His hand is stretched out,
>   and who will turn it back?

ISAIAH 14:27

> For I am God, and there is no other;
>   I am God, and there is none like me,
> declaring the end from the beginning
>   and from ancient times things not yet done,

saying, "My counsel shall stand,
*   and I will accomplish all my purpose."*
ISAIAH 46:9-10

All the inhabitants of the earth are accounted as nothing,
*   and he does according to his will among the host of heaven*
*   and among the inhabitants of the earth;*
and none can stay his hand
*   or say to him, "What have you done?"*
DANIEL 4:35

Come now, you who say, "Today or tomorrow we will go into
such and such a town and spend a year there and trade and
make a profit"—yet you do not know what tomorrow will
bring. What is your life? For you are a mist that appears for a
little time and then vanishes. Instead you ought to say, "If the
Lord wills, we will live and do this or that."
JAMES 4:13-15

So we see that God does as He wills, and we can do nothing except what He wills. This would be terrifying if that were all we knew about God. But God is not only sovereign; He is perfect in His unfailing love and infinite in His wisdom, which is far beyond our ability to understand.

Submission to God's providence, then, means we recognize that there is yet much work to be done in our character. God uses adversities as one means of doing that work (see Hebrews 12:5-11). It means that we accept the difficult and painful events of life, even those brought about by the actions of other people, as under the controlling hand of our loving and infinitely wise heavenly Father. It means we believe that God causes all events in our lives, whether good or bad as we judge them, to work together to conform us more and more into the likeness of Christ (Romans 8:28-29). It means that we give thanks in all circumstances (1 Thessalonians 5:18)—not for the circumstance considered in itself, but for God's promise to use these circumstances to conform us more to Christ.

I confess that giving thanks in all circumstances is a challenge for me these days. Among other things, at the age of eighty-six I am dealing with several significant health issues that make life increasingly difficult. So how do I give thanks in these situations?

I mentioned above that God causes all our circumstances to work together to conform us more to Christ. That's great for the future, but what about today, when I am experiencing one of those inconveniences? For this I go to the latter part of Hebrews 13:5, where God promises, "I will never leave you nor forsake you." In the Greek this is an emphatic statement. It is as if God is saying, "*No!* I will never leave you. *No!* I will never forsake you."

So I pray something like this: "God, this is a very difficult time for me, but you have promised two things: first, that you will not forsake me in this situation; and second, that in your infinite wisdom you will use this difficult circumstance to conform me more to the image of Christ."

I probably will never know how He does this, or even what the specific result will be. But God really does mean what He says. Several months ago I was chafing under some difficult providence of God. The thought came into my mind, almost as if God were speaking, "Which would you rather I do: remove this difficult circumstance, or use it to conform you more to the image of My Son?" Through that thought God gave me the meekness to accept what He was doing.

So far in this chapter we have considered the blessing of meekness toward God. The other aspect of Jesus' teaching here is meekness toward other people. The Puritan Thomas Watson wrote that meekness toward other people consists of three things: the bearing of injuries, the forgiving of injuries, and the returning of good for evil.[1] Let's analyze what these three expressions of meekness look like in everyday life.

Bearing of injuries is a response with meekness to the hurts of other people. It may be unjust criticism, unkind gossip, or even slander. It may be that, in speaking to you, someone puts you down. It may be that you are passed over for a promotion in favor of someone clearly less deserving. There are numerous ways people can hurt us.

What does meekness look like in these situations? Peter helps us when he said of Jesus,

> When he was reviled, he did not revile in return; when he suffered, he did not threaten, but continued entrusting himself to him who judges justly.
>
> I PETER 2:23

Some readers may think I am advocating "doormat" Christianity, where we allow people to run roughshod over us. There are Christian responses to keep this from happening, but we have to balance these with the fact that Jesus was the ultimate "doormat": He allowed Himself to be crucified by wicked men.

One of the greatest tests of our meekness is the way we deal with the hurts dealt to us by other people. So instead of harboring resentment toward them, let us entrust ourselves to God who causes all these hurts to work together for our good.

The second expression of meekness is *forgiving the injuries or sins of others*. The classic passage of Scripture on forgiving others is the parable of the unforgiving servant found in Matthew 18:23-35; we are going to look at this passage in depth in chapter 6. But for now consider the following Scriptures:

- "Be kind to one another, tenderhearted, forgiving one another, as God in Christ forgave you" (Ephesians 4:32). So we are to forgive as God in Christ forgave us.
- "If one has a complaint against another, forgiving each other; as the Lord has forgiven you, so you also must forgive" (Colossians 3:13).

Ephesians and Colossians were written at about the same time, so it is not surprising that Paul would write essentially the same thing regarding forgiveness in both letters. However, in Colossians he adds the words, "so you also must forgive." The truth I hope you will see is that in both of the above Scriptures, our forgiving one another is linked to our forgiveness from God.

This idea takes us back to the first character trait in the Beatitudes, "poor in spirit." Our willingness to forgive others is proportional to our realization, in the depths of our hearts, of how much we have been forgiven by God. If we are comfortable in our decent lifestyle because we do not commit the flagrant sins of our society, and if we do not see much need for continual forgiveness, then we are not likely to readily forgive others when they sin against us.

Those who are "poor in spirit," however, recognize more and more how much sin and corruption is still present in their hearts. They recognize that though they have been given a new heart (Ezekiel 36:26), their heart is still deceitful (Jeremiah 17:9), and the flesh, or sinful nature, that still dwells in them strives against the Spirit within us every day (Galatians 5:17).

Now we need to go back to Paul's words in Colossians 3:13: "So you also must forgive." In effect, Paul is saying that we don't have a choice: Because we have been forgiven so much, we have an obligation to forgive those who sin against us. Yet our motive for forgiving should not be our obligation but the realization of how much we have been forgiven.

I think of Paul's letter to his dear friend Philemon, written at about the same time he wrote Ephesians and Colossians. Philemon was no doubt wealthy, for his house was large enough to accommodate a church. Philemon also had a slave, Onesimus, who apparently had run away but ended up meeting Paul in Rome. Paul led him to Christ; in Philemon 1:10 he refers to Onesimus as "my child . . . whose father I became in my imprisonment."

Paul had a sticky problem. He knew Onesimus needed to return to Philemon, but he desired that Philemon not only forgive Onesimus but receive him "as a beloved brother" (verse 16).

Paul's letter appears in our Bibles as "the letter of Paul to Philemon." Notice how he handles his request, in verses 8-9:

> *Though I am bold enough in Christ to command you to do what is required, yet for love's sake I prefer to appeal to you—I, Paul, an old man and now a prisoner also for Christ Jesus.*

In effect Paul says, "I could command you to do what is right, Philemon. You really have no choice but to forgive Onesimus."

Paul is saying, "You have a duty to forgive. To not forgive would be a sin against God." But then Paul adds, "Yet for love's sake I prefer to appeal to you." Paul wants Philemon to *want* to do what he *must* do.

Reading between the lines, it appears that Onesimus had not only run away but had also stolen in the process. So Paul writes in verses 18-19,

> *If he has wronged you at all, or owes you anything, charge that to my account. I, Paul, write this with my own hand: I will repay it—to say nothing of your owing me even your own self.*

These are touching words. Paul, in prison, says, "charge that to my account." This is what Jesus says to the Father: "Charge Jerry's sin to my account"—and He paid for it all through His death on the cross. Paul says, "I will repay it," but he then reminds Philemon that Philemon owes even his own self to Paul (an acknowledgment that Paul led him to Christ). And so we owe our salvation entirely to Christ, who says to us, "Forgive as I have forgiven you" (see Ephesians 4:32).

This private and very personal letter from Paul to Philemon is more than just a letter. It is a part of the divinely inspired Scriptures. It is the very Word of God, and God providentially directed church councils to include it in the canon of Scripture for a reason. It serves as an illustration in a small way of what God has done for us through Christ.

Consider what we were. Paul says in Ephesians 2:1-3 that we were dead in our sins, that effectively we were slaves to the world, to the devil, and to the desires of our passions. Furthermore, we were by nature objects of God's wrath. This is a far worse predicament than that of Onesimus. But God, who is rich in mercy, not only forgave us our enormous moral debt that stood against us (Colossians 2:13-14). He also "raised us up with Him and seated us with Him in the heavenly places" (Ephesians 2:6).

So we are to forgive as God forgave us. This is the command of God. But again, God wants us to forgive for love's sake, not because we are commanded to do so. And the only thing that will motivate us to forgive for love's sake is to be "poor in spirit" and recognize how much God has forgiven us.

The third area of meekness toward others is *returning good for evil*. The classic passage on this is Romans 12:14-21:

- "Bless those who persecute you; bless and do not curse them" (verse 14).
- "Repay no one evil for evil, but give thought to do what is honorable" (verse 17).
- "Beloved, never avenge yourselves, but leave it to the wrath of God, for it is written, 'Vengeance is mine, I will repay, says the Lord'" (verse 19).

Very few of us in the West experience actual persecution today (see chapter 9). So in order to apply these instructions in our present-day culture, we need to restate the word *persecute* to mean anything that is done to harm us, to slander us, to defraud us, or to block our path to a promotion—anything that is damaging to us. And Paul's instruction to us is to bless and not curse those who do these things.

One of the best ways to bless people is to pray for them. Often the perpetrators of these hurtful or harmful acts are fellow believers, so we can pray that God will bless them as we would want Him to bless us. If they are unbelievers, we can pray that God will draw them to believe in the gospel and trust Christ for salvation.

We certainly do not want to repay evil for evil. We don't want to slander someone who has slandered us. Sad to say, this sometimes occurs in some of our churches, when unsubstantiated accusations are made back and forth.

Above all, we should never seek to avenge ourselves of wrong by doing evil to someone else. As I've thought about Paul's admonitions in Romans 12, I've concluded that we do most of our harm to each other with our speech rather than our actions. So let us take to heart Paul's instruction in Ephesians 4:29:

> *Let no corrupting talk come out of your mouths, but only such as is good for building up, as fits the occasion, that it may give grace to those who hear.*

Note the two absolutes in Paul's words:

- *No* corrupting talk.
- *Only* such as is good for building up.

Paul also says in Titus 3:2, "Speak evil of no one." This applies even to those who by their words have hurt us in some way.

You can see that meekness truly is humility in action. It takes humility to submit ourselves to and be convicted by God's Word. It takes humility to not murmur or complain about the difficult and painful events in life, but instead to see them as God's work of growing us more and more into the likeness of Christ. It takes humility to bear with and forgive those who hurt us in some way. And it certainly takes humility to repay evil with good. In summary I again quote John Blanchard:

Meekness is a defining grace, produced by the Holy Spirit in the life of the Christian, which characterizes that person's response towards God and man. Meekness towards God is a spirit of submission to all of God's dealings with us, especially those which cause us sorrow or pain, in the settled conviction that in all of these he is graciously, wisely and sovereignly working "for the good of those who love him" (Romans 8:28). Meekness towards man means bearing patiently with the hurtful actions of others and dealing gently with their failures, not only in the assurance that all of these are under God's providential control, but in the knowledge that, left to ourselves, we have no claim to be any stronger than the weakest of our friends or any better than the worst of our enemies."[2]

CHAPTER FIVE

HUNGER AND THIRST FOR RIGHTEOUSNESS

Blessed are those who hunger and thirst for
righteousness, for they shall be satisfied.

MATTHEW 5:6

In the first two Beatitudes Jesus uses the strongest words possible: The Greek word for *poor* refers to abject poverty; the word for *mourn* is what we do when a loved one dies.

Now we come to another set of strong words, *hunger* and *thirst*. Jesus did not say, "Blessed are those who are hungry and thirsty," but rather "those who hunger and thirst." Both words express an intense desire, similar to that shown in the following verses:

> *O God, you are my God; earnestly I seek you;*
> *my soul thirsts for you;*
> *my flesh faints for you,*
> *as in a dry and weary land where there is no water.*
> PSALM 63:1

> *Call out for insight*
> *and raise your voice for understanding, . . .*

> *seek it like silver*
> *and search for it as for hidden treasures.*

PROVERBS 2:3-4

> *My soul yearns for you in the night;*
> *my spirit within me earnestly seeks you.*
> *For when your judgments are in the earth,*
> *the inhabitants of the world learn righteousness.*

ISAIAH 26:9

To hunger and thirst for righteousness, then, indicates a strong overwhelming desire for righteousness. This leads to the question, "What is righteousness?"

Righteousness denotes the state of being right. Biblically, it means perfect accord with God's law in every way: thought, word, deed, and even motive. Paul expressed this absolute accord in Galatians 3:10:

> *For all who rely on works of the law are under a curse; for*
> *it is written, "Cursed be everyone who does not abide by all*
> *things written in the Book of the Law, and do them."*

The word *all* that Paul uses means "without exception." This is the kind of righteousness that we are to hunger and thirst after: to live in perfect accord with the law of God.

None of us can do this, so we may well ask, "Why hunger for something that is impossible to attain? Isn't that an exercise in futility?" Paul plainly declares, "None is righteous, no, not one" (Romans 3:10), and again, in Romans 3:20, "For by works of the law no human being will be justified in his sight, since through the law comes knowledge of sin." (The word *justified* here means "to be declared righteous.") So again we ask the question, "Why hunger and thirst after that which is unattainable?"

The answer lies in the twofold meaning of righteousness in the Bible. First is a righteousness that God requires, that is, perfect obedience to His law. This is the implication of Galatians 3:10, which we have seen above. No one measures up to that law—that is, no one except the Lord Jesus Christ. His own self-assessment was, "I always do the things that are pleasing to [God]" (John 8:29).

The four major writers of the New Testament letters—Paul, Peter, John, and the writer of Hebrews—are unanimous in their assertion that Jesus was perfectly righteous: that is, perfectly obedient to the law of God (see 2 Corinthians 5:21; Hebrews 4:15; 1 Peter 2:22; and 1 John 3:5). Keep in mind that these four writers were writing under the direct guidance of the Holy Spirit (see 2 Peter 1:21), so they were writing exactly what God wanted them to write. So this is God's testimony about Jesus: He was totally without sin. Or to put it in the positive sense, He was totally righteous. For thirty-three years He lived out that which is impossible for us to attain, and what He did, He did as the divinely appointed representative of all who trust in Him for salvation. Therefore, because we are united to Christ we are considered by God to be as righteous as Christ Himself.

But what about our personal failure to live a perfectly righteous life? We have already seen that no one is righteous, so what happens to our sin, our failure to perfectly obey the law of God? Does our sin just vanish into thin air? Or does God sweep our sins under some cosmic rug?

The answer is no. God's justice demands a just payment, and Jesus took care of that also through His death on the cross, where He bore the just and holy wrath of God that our sin deserves. As Paul wrote in 2 Corinthians 5:21, "[God] made him to be sin." Then, as Peter wrote, "He himself bore our sins in his body on the tree" (1 Peter 2:24). Perhaps the greatest statement on the truth of Jesus bearing our sins is Isaiah 53:5-6:

> *But he was pierced for our transgressions;*
> *he was crushed for our iniquities;*
> *upon him was the chastisement that brought us peace,*
> *and with his wounds we are healed.*
> *All we like sheep have gone astray;*
> *we have turned—every one—to his own way;*
> *and the LORD has laid on him*
> *the iniquity of us all.*

Jesus perfectly satisfied the righteous requirements of God's law, both in its precepts (what God requires of us) and in its penalty for our failure to perfectly obey. As is often said, "He lived a life we could not live, and died a death we deserved to die." As a result, all who trust in Christ as Savior are justified—that is, counted and treated by God as perfectly righteous.

We might call this righteousness "positional righteousness." That is, our position or standing before God is one of perfect righteousness, as righteous as Christ Himself. At the moment we trusted Christ as Savior, we were justified—declared by God to be righteous. You will never be more or less righteous before God any day of your life than you were the moment you trusted Christ as your Savior.

This raises another question: Why should I hunger and thirst for that which I already have? The answer is that the more we grow and mature in the Christian life, the more sensitive we become to the sin and failure we see in our lives. It is not that we necessarily sin more but rather that we become more aware of and mourn over the sin that is already there. As that happens, we hunger more and more after the righteousness we have only in Christ.

I mentioned in the previous chapter my ongoing challenge to give thanks in all circumstances. This really came to the fore a few weeks ago when I couldn't get some information I needed from my computer. Somewhat frustrated, I turned to my cell phone to enter a new number, and for some reason the screen for doing that would not come up. Giving up, I decided to go water some newly planted plants, but I could not find the spray nozzle I had used only the day before. By this time I was thoroughly frustrated and grumpy, and in no mood to give thanks.

My attitude was sinful: We are to "give thanks in all circumstances; *for this is the will of God* in Christ Jesus for you" (1 Thessalonians 5:18, emphasis added). Paul uses an almost identical expression in 1 Thessalonians 4:3: "For this is the will of God . . . that you abstain from sexual immorality." It is the will of God that I abstain from sexual immorality, and it is the will of God that I give thanks in all circumstances.

I knew my attitude that day was sinful, and that my only remedy was in the righteousness of Christ. So I went to God, confessed my sin, and by faith laid hold of the righteousness I have in Christ. I hungered and thirsted that day after Christ's righteousness.

There is a legitimate sense in which we are to hunger and thirst for that perfect righteousness we already have in Christ. This should be a continual daily attitude of all growing Christians because we continue to sin every day. The gospel—the Good News of what God has done for us in Christ—is like the manna God provided for the Israelites in the wilderness. It had to be gathered daily and could not be stored up (Exodus 16:16-21). In a similar sense, we need to appropriate the Good News every day as we see ourselves continuing to sin every day.

The first line of that great old hymn "The Solid Rock" is, "My hope is built on nothing less than Jesus' blood and righteousness." This should be true not only for our hope of eternal salvation but also for our hope for God's favor and blessing on our lives today. It is in this sense that we should hunger and thirst for that which we already have in Christ.

There is a second righteousness that we should hunger and thirst for: the experiential righteousness we are to pursue every day. God has inextricably linked together the righteousness we have in Christ and the righteousness we should pursue. He does not give one without the other. Therefore, whoever hungers and thirsts after the righteousness we have in Christ will also hunger and thirst to be righteous in his or her daily experience.

Paul wrote in 2 Corinthians 5:17 that if anyone is in Christ (positionally righteous), he is a new creation. This new creation is biased toward pursuing experiential righteousness. This radical change in our hearts and minds is best described in Ezekiel 36:26-27:

> *And I will give you a new heart, and a new spirit I will put within you. And I will remove the heart of stone from your flesh and give you a heart of flesh. And I will put my Spirit within you, and cause you to walk in my statutes and be careful to obey my rules.*

In this Scripture God promises two things: to give us a new heart, and to put His Spirit within us—to give life to the new heart, enabling us to pursue righteousness in our daily lives.

Along with God's promises, we have the clear teaching of Scripture that we are to pursue this righteousness. Consider the following passages, all having to do with our experiential righteousness:

> *So flee youthful passions and pursue righteousness, faith, love, and peace, along with those who call on the Lord from a pure heart.*
>
> 2 TIMOTHY 2:22

> *He himself bore our sins in his body on the tree, that we might die to sin and live to righteousness. By his wounds you have been healed.*
>
> I PETER 2:24

> *By this it is evident who are the children of God, and who are the children of the devil: whoever does not practice righteousness is not of God, nor is the one who does not love his brother.*
>
> I JOHN 3:10

We could add to this list Hebrews 12:14: "Strive for peace with everyone, and for the holiness without which no one will see the Lord." The words *holiness* and *righteousness* are closely related and sometimes used interchangeably. So we are to pursue righteousness, we are to live to righteousness, we are to practice righteousness, and we are to strive for it.

It is clear from Scripture, then, that we are to pursue an experiential righteousness. But what will cause us to hunger and thirst for it? The answer is twofold.

First, as we have already observed, the new nature is inclined by the Holy Spirit to pursue righteousness. This may be only a small spark in a new believer, but as he or she grows spiritually, this hunger will increase.

The second motivation is gratitude for the righteousness we have in Christ. The more we pursue experiential righteousness, the more we see how far short we come in attaining it. This causes us to be more appreciative of the righteousness we have in Christ, thus producing the gratitude that motivates us to pursue experiential righteousness.

If God has commanded us to pursue experiential righteousness, and if we hunger and thirst to do so, what does day-to-day experiential righteousness look like? Basically, it is obedience to the moral commands of the Bible, as the Holy Spirit brings them to our attention. Obviously He does not bring them to our attention all at once. Like physical growth, spiritual growth is slow, incremental, and often hardly observable. In my own experience, it seems the Holy Spirit focuses on one or two areas of need at a time. Right now, as I have mentioned, His focus for me seems to be on more consistent giving of thanks in all circumstances, even the difficult ones.

"As the Holy Spirit brings them to our attention" implies regular exposure to the Bible through our reading or studying it, as well as hearing it taught by our pastors or other spiritual leaders. There will be no growth in experiential righteousness apart from a regular intake of the Word of God.

As we begin to look for practical expressions of righteousness, we may find it overwhelming. We think, *How can I perfectly obey all of these commands?* The venerable Heidelberg Catechism, similar in nature and doctrine to the better-known

Westminster Catechisms, asks a similar question: "Can those who are converted to God keep these commandments perfectly?" (Question 114). The Catechism then gives the following answer:

> No, but even the holiest men, while in this life, have only a small beginning of this obedience; yet so, that with earnest purpose they begin to live not only according to some but to all the commandments of God.

Note that it says that "even the holiest men, while in this life, have only a small beginning of this obedience." But they are not satisfied with this small beginning. Rather, they hunger and thirst after the righteousness they know is unattainable.

On the wall of the auto shop where I take my car to be serviced is a large sign with these words, "Perfection is unattainable, but if we aim for it we will achieve excellence." The principle expressed in that sign is a good one for us. The perfect righteousness that we pursue is unattainable in this life. But if we hunger and thirst for it and diligently pursue it, over time we will grow more and more into the person God wants us to be.

There is one other important truth that I stated in chapter 2 but that needs to be constantly repeated and believed. We are absolutely dependent on the Holy Spirit to work in us Himself and to enable us to work. We cannot make one inch of progress toward experiential righteousness without His divine enablement. Amen!

Our hunger and thirst for the righteousness we have in Christ and our hunger and thirst for experiential righteousness grow together. The realization of the righteousness we have in Christ motivates us to live up to that righteousness, which we are to pursue but will never completely attain. Our inability to attain true righteousness in our experience drives us back to the righteousness we have in Christ.

How do these two aspects of hunger and thirst after righteousness produce humility? Only those who are poor in spirit and who mourn over sin will hunger and thirst after the righteousness we have in Christ. And only those who are poor in spirit will recognize how far short they come in attaining experiential righteousness. The awareness of our absolute dependence on the righteousness of Christ and of our failure to attain more experiential righteousness will produce humility in us.

So we constantly go back to the character trait of the first Beatitude, "poverty in spirit." This is where humility begins, and it is this honest self-evaluation that will produce both the humility of hunger and thirst after righteousness that we have in Christ, and also the experiential righteousness we are to pursue.

CHAPTER SIX

MERCIFUL

Blessed are the merciful,
for they shall receive mercy.

MATTHEW 5:7

I was sitting in our city's downtown library reading a book while I waited for my wife, who was attending a meeting. As I sat there, homeless men began to come in, apparently looking for a warm spot on a cold, windy night. All of them were unkempt and, yes, a bit smelly. My reaction was, *What are these dirty, smelly men doing in our nice middle-class library?*

I was not merciful that night. In fact, I was unmerciful.

The first four character traits of the Beatitudes—poverty in spirit, mourning, meekness, and hungering and thirsting after righteousness—all address our internal character and our relationship to God. Here in this Beatitude, "Blessed are the merciful," Jesus began to address our relationship with other people.

There are three words that are very close in meaning, in both Greek and English. The English words are *mercy*, *pity*, and *compassion*, and they seem to be used somewhat interchangeably. However, the word Jesus used in Matthew 5:7, translated as *merciful* in our English Bibles, is stronger than *pity* or *compassion*; it denotes not only feelings but action.

49

We see this in Jesus' familiar parable of the Good Samaritan (Luke 10:30-37). In answer to a lawyer's question—"And who is my neighbor?" (verse 29)—Jesus told this parable about a man who had been beaten and robbed. In the parable, a priest and a Levite ignored the beaten man, but the Good Samaritan "had compassion" (verse 33). He then went on to put his compassion into *action* (verses 34-35):

> *He went to him and bound up his wounds, pouring*
> *on oil and wine. Then he set him on his own animal*
> *and brought him to an inn and took care of him.*
> *And the next day he took out two denarii and gave*
> *them to the innkeeper, saying, "Take care of him,*
> *and whatever more you spend, I will repay you when*
> *I come back."*

After telling the parable, Jesus asked the lawyer, "Which of these three, do you think, proved to be a neighbor to the man who fell among the robbers?" (verse 36). The lawyer answered, "The one who showed him mercy" (verse 37).

Note the subtle distinction between compassion and mercy. The Samaritan *had* compassion and then *showed* mercy.

Mercy expresses itself in two general areas: In the temporal sense, mercy seeks to meet the physical needs of others, as the Good Samaritan did in Jesus' parable. The second way mercy expresses itself is granting forgiveness to those who have sinned against us. This is an important expression of mercy, and we will address it, but first let's consider what the Bible says about showing compassion and mercy to those in need.

Provision for the poor was part of the Old Testament law. Leviticus 19:9-10 says,

> *When you reap the harvest of your land, you shall not reap your field right up to its edge, neither shall you gather the gleanings after your harvest. And you shall not strip your vineyard bare, neither shall you gather the fallen grapes of your vineyard. You shall leave them for the poor and for the sojourner: I am the LORD your God.*

Psalm 41:1 says,

> *Blessed is the one who considers the poor!*
>   *In the day of trouble the LORD delivers him.*

Again we see concern for the poor addressed in Isaiah 58:7, 10:

> *Is [fasting] not to share your bread with the hungry*
>   *and bring the homeless poor into your house;*
> *when you see the naked, to cover him,*
>   *and not to hide yourself from your own flesh? . . .*
> *If you pour yourself out for the hungry*
>   *and satisfy the desire of the afflicted,*
> *then shall your light rise in the darkness*
>   *and your gloom be as the noonday.*

The apostle Paul addresses this principle in Galatians 6:9-10:

> *And let us not grow weary of doing good, for in due season we will reap, if we do not give up. So then, as we have opportunity, let us do good to everyone, and especially to those who are of the household of faith.*

The most significant section of Scripture on the subject of giving is 2 Corinthians 8–9. When we teach on the general subject of giving, most of us use these two chapters as foundational passages on both the motivation and practical expressions of giving. While we often apply these principles to giving to our church or mission organizations, Paul actually wrote these chapters to encourage the Corinthian believers to give to people they had never met: the poor saints in Jerusalem who were suffering persecution because of their trust in Jesus.

We see, then, that there is abundant evidence in both the Old and New Testaments that we are to be merciful and compassionate to those in need, whether at home or abroad. So when Jesus said, "Blessed are the merciful," surely He would have had in mind mercy to those who are physically poor or needy.

But what about the *spiritual* needs of the poor and needy? Suppose we were able, by the generous giving of all Christians, to raise multitudes of men, women, and children out of abject poverty into a livable and decent standard of living. If we were to do that to the neglect of their eternal destiny, we would have done them a fatal disservice. As Jesus said, "For what does it profit a man to gain the whole world and forfeit his soul? For what can a man give in return for his soul?" (Mark 8:36-37).

During a number of years in the early to mid-twentieth century, there arose an unnecessary dichotomy between the physical and the spiritual needs of people. Many liberal churches abandoned the biblical gospel in favor of what was called the "social gospel," or meeting the physical needs of the poor and needy. Unfortunately, many evangelical churches, fearful of drifting in that direction, abandoned all efforts to meet the physical needs of people. Clearly the Bible does not support such distinctions. Rather, we are to address both physical and spiritual needs.

Peter and John are good examples of this. On their way to

the temple they encountered a man, crippled from birth, who asked alms of them. Peter responded,

> *"I have no silver and gold, but what I do have I give to you.*
> *In the name of Jesus Christ of Nazareth, rise up and walk!"*
> *And he took him by the right hand and raised him up,*
> *and immediately his feet and ankles were made strong.*
> ACTS 3:6-7

Peter's response has become a well-known and classic statement through the centuries. Some have misused his words as a rationale for meeting only the physical needs of people; but the fact is, although Peter did heal the man's feet and ankles—meeting his most apparent physical need—he did it in the name of Jesus Christ of Nazareth. Later in the temple, he used the man's healing as an occasion to preach the gospel (Acts 3:11-26). For Peter and John, there was no separation between the true gospel and the physical needs of the crippled man.

The greatest expression of mercy is God's forgiveness of our sins and bringing us into His kingdom. We saw in chapter 4 that Paul describes us as having been spiritually dead, slaves, and objects of God's wrath (Ephesians 2:1-3). We were not just undeserving of God's favor. We were ill-deserving. We justly deserved God's wrath.

Then Paul uses one of his favorite words of contrast: "But God, being rich in mercy" (Ephesians 2:4). God is described as a merciful God in numerous Old Testament Scripture passages (see, for example, Exodus 34:6; Nehemiah 9:31; Psalm 103:8; 145:8). These expressions of God's mercy are all in the context of our sin and God's judgment. And we are to show mercy in the light of God's mercy to us.

I promised in chapter 4 that we would address the classic passage on forgiveness as an expression of mercy. That is the parable of the unmerciful servant, Matthew 18:23-35. The occasion of the parable is Peter's question to Jesus, "Lord, how often will my brother sin against me, and I forgive him? As many as seven times?" (verse 21).

Jesus said to him, "I do not say to you seven times, but seventy-seven times" (verse 22). Essentially, as often as you are sinned against, you are to forgive.

Then Jesus tells the story of a servant who owed his master ten thousand talents (about 6 billion dollars today). The servant was not able to pay, and out of pity, the master forgave him that debt. But when that servant went away, he saw a fellow servant who owed him a hundred denarii (about $12,000 today). The fellow servant pleaded for patience from the first servant, but that servant refused. Now $12,000 is not a little sum, but compared to $6,000,000,000, it is a trifle.

The point of the parable is that we are all ten-thousand-talent debtors to God. Not a day passes without each of us sinning many times a day, either in thought, word, deed, or motive. The reason we do not recognize this is that we think of sin only in terms of the flagrant sins out in society. We do not see our impatience, our short bursts of anger, or our verbal put-downs of other people as sin.

Moreover, the magnitude of our sin is not measured by its effects on other people but by its assault upon the infinite majesty and holiness of God. However grievous another person's sin against us is, or how often they sin against us, we are to forgive because we have been forgiven such an enormous debt of sin by God. Furthermore, as Jesus said at the end of the parable (verse 35), <u>we are to forgive from our hearts</u>—not <u>superficially but genuinely</u>—as we consider how much we have <u>been forgiven.</u>

Note the consequences of not forgiving in the parable. The master was angry with the servant, in fact calling him wicked, and delivered him over to the jailers. This is a parable, and not every detail can be likened to real life, so we cannot describe what being delivered over to the jailer might have looked like in real life. But it does teach us the seriousness of not forgiving those who sin against us.

This parable raises the question, what does it mean to forgive? Consider the following Scriptures:

> *I, I am he*
> *who blots out your transgressions for my own sake,*
> *and I will not remember your sins.*
>
> ISAIAH 43:25

> *For I will be merciful toward their iniquities,*
> *and I will remember their sins no more.*
>
> HEBREWS 8:12

> *"I will remember their sins and their lawless deeds no more."*
> *Where there is forgiveness of these, there is no longer any*
> *offering for sin.*
>
> HEBREWS 10:17-18

The common thought in all three Scriptures is that God no longer remembers our sins. He blots them out, and He never brings them up again.

This is what it means to forgive. We do not remember the sins against us. Someone has pointed out the difference between forgetting and not remembering. We unintentionally forget lots of things—where we put our car keys, and other things like that—but we choose not to remember. We can choose not to replay in our minds the sin of someone else against us. We can choose not to bring up that sin again—either to ourselves, to another person, or to the person who sinned against us. To bring it up again indicates that we have not truly forgiven, or else that we are still struggling to forgive and need to continue working on it, asking God to help us.

Forgiveness usually is not simply an event at one point in time. Even if we have said, "I forgive you," we often struggle to forgive. Usually the hurts which necessitate forgiveness don't go away so easily, and we must keep choosing not to remember them.

There is another truth we need to see in order to understand forgiveness. When the master in the parable forgave that enormous debt of ten thousand talents, his net worth was immediately reduced by about 6 billion dollars in today's currency. The cost to God of forgiving us cannot be measured by money; it is measured in the death of his Son on the cross to pay for our sins. It is an immeasurable cost.

Forgiving costs us. It means we let go of our hurt and resentment and never bring it up again, even to ourselves. And if the offending person is a believer, this means we pray for them, for Jesus said, "But I say to you, Love your enemies and pray for those who persecute you" (Matthew 5:44). If the offender is an unbeliever, we should pray for his or her salvation.

We have seen the importance of being merciful in both the physical and spiritual realms. How do these two expressions of mercy show humility in action?

Remember my reaction to the homeless men in the library. I was prideful. How dare these men invade our nice, middle-class space? Humility would have genuinely said, "There but for the grace of God go I." Humility would have thought, *Is there anything I can do to help these men?* Humility would have recognized that it is the Lord who makes some poor and some rich (or in our case, middle-class). It is the Lord who brings low and who exalts (1 Samuel 2:7). If I am any better off economically or socially than these homeless men, it is all due to the grace of God.

God did convict me of my unmerciful attitude, and I began to think of how my wife and I might show mercy to them. Since at my age I do not have the physical ability to get directly involved, we began to contribute significantly to our local rescue mission, which provides shelter and meals to the homeless in our city.

But the real expression of humility in action comes in forgiving others when they have sinned against us in some way. To forgive others means we regard ourselves as ten-thousand-talent debtors. It means we extend mercy because we have received mercy from God (see Matthew 18:33). Again we see that merciful people are those who are poor in spirit, recognizing that they are not better (and perhaps even worse) than those who sin against them. So as I have said earlier, humility in action begins with being poor in spirit. All the succeeding character traits flow out of that one.

CHAPTER SEVEN

PURE IN HEART

Blessed are the pure in heart,
for they shall see God.

MATTHEW 5:8

For many years I assumed that "pure in heart" referred to moral or sexual purity. It certainly includes that, but it means much more.

To better understand what it means to be pure in heart, it will help to see the different ways the Bible uses the word *heart*. In addition to the physical function of the organ in our chest, John Blanchard lists eight functions of the heart identified in the Scriptures:

- It is the seat of the emotions.
- It is the seat of understanding.
- It is the seat of reason.
- It is associated with the conscience.
- It is the seat of motives.
- It is the root of our desires.
- It is involved in decision making.
- It is the seat of faith.[1]

We can see, then, that the heart stands for one's inner being, the "real you," that which makes you who you are.

The word *pure* is used of clothing that has been washed, of grain from which all chaff has been removed, and of gold that has been refined until all impurities have been removed. A pure heart, then, is one from which all sinful desires have been removed. Positively it means to love God with all my heart, soul, and mind (Matthew 22:37). It means to live all of life to the glory of God (1 Corinthians 10:31).

Here we encounter a problem. As we see from its eight distinct functions, the spiritual heart is very complex. Each of us can be enticed to sin through any of these inclinations. Furthermore, our hearts are deceitful and searchable by God alone. We cannot plumb the depths of our motives. We may desire to glorify God, but in our heart we want to look good in the process. In our decision making, we may rationalize an action we know is not consistent with the will of God. Our understanding and our reasoning are often clouded by our desires. If we are honest, then, we have to admit we do not have a pure heart.

So how does one grow in purity of heart? I believe it begins by accepting the lordship of Christ in our lives. What does that mean?

Sometimes the lordship of Christ has been taught by using a car illustration. You are driving along in the car of your life with Jesus in the passenger seat. At some point Jesus says, "I want to drive." So you turn over the driving of your life to Him. In doing so, you acknowledge His lordship over your life.

In recent years I have concluded that this driving illustration is insufficient to picture the lordship of Christ. Closer to the truth is that Christ does not say, "I want to drive" but rather

"I own this car." Paul puts it this way: "You are not your own, for you were bought with a price" (1 Corinthians 6:19-20).

To grasp the truth that we no longer belong to ourselves but to Christ is to grasp a truth fundamental to the Christian life. It is also to understand in a practical sense what it means to be pure in heart.

Another illustration will perhaps more forcibly drive home the ownership of Christ over our lives. Suppose I sell you a piece of commercial property on which I am already behind in my mortgage payments. You not only pay me a fair price for the property but also pay my overdue payments. Now the property belongs totally to you. I no longer have a say in how the property is used. This is essentially what Christ has done. By His death on the cross He paid our debt to God, a debt we could not possibly pay ourselves. As Paul says in Titus 2:14, "[He] gave himself for us to redeem us from all lawlessness and to purify for himself a people for his own possession who are zealous for good works."

This doesn't mean Jesus wants you to ask Him what color socks you should wear today. It does mean He wants you to constantly keep in mind that you are not your own. You were bought with a price. You are His possession.

Once we acknowledge God's ownership of us, our responsibility becomes clear: Whatever we do must serve God's purposes. And central among God's purposes, as demonstrated throughout the Scriptures, is God's glory. Paul concludes a brief message on sexual purity with the admonition, "So glorify God in your body" (1 Corinthians 6:20). He does the same in 1 Corinthians 10:31 after a discussion of the issue of eating meat offered to idols. "Whatever you do, do all to the glory of God." That, positively, is purity of heart.

Years ago, while still in my twenties, I was given a book titled *Have We No Rights?*[2] I could not finish the book because the author's answer was "No, we have no rights," and at that stage of my Christian life I could not accept that. Now I agree with her. I have no rights because I no longer "own" myself. I have no right to good health, though I am responsible for living prudently with regard to health. I have no right to success in life, though I am responsible for pursuing excellence in whatever work God calls me to. I have no right to be treated with fairness and dignity, though I am responsible for treating others with fairness and dignity (see Matthew 7:12; 22:39).

That last statement seems unfair, doesn't it? The answer to that apparent unfairness is that the Lord Jesus Christ now holds that right to my life, and He exercises it with perfect love and wisdom in such a way that good or bad treatment by others will be used to make me more like Him.

Now let's go back to the car illustration with Jesus having said, "I own this car." I still drive the car, but I recognize His ownership, so now my objective is no longer to drive where I want to go but only to drive where He wants to go. To apply the illustration to real life: I still live my life. I still use my understanding and reasoning abilities. I still have emotions, motives, and desires. But to be pure in heart—or better, to seek to be pure in heart—I must bring all those activities of the heart under the ownership of Christ.

This idea of Jesus being the "owner" of our lives is a radical idea to our independently minded society today—even Christian society. Many Christians are not sure they like the idea. They are happy to live a "decent Christian life" and avoid major sins, but to give up control of their lives to Christ is a different matter. What will motivate Christians to do this? The answer lies in our grasp of the love of Christ for us, as it is revealed in the gospel. The Jesus who "owns" us is the Jesus who died in our place to save us from the just and holy wrath of God.

One of my favorite passages of Scripture is 2 Corinthians 5:14-15:

> *For the love of Christ controls us, because we have concluded this: that one has died for all, therefore all have died; and he died for all, that those who live might no longer live for themselves but for him who for their sake died and was raised.*

What does Paul mean when he says the love of Christ controls us? Some years ago Kenneth Wuest, a lecturer in Greek at Moody Bible Institute, wrote an expanded translation of the New Testament. This is how he translated 2 Corinthians 5:14-15:

> *For the love which Christ has [for me] presses on me from all sides, holding me to one end and prohibiting me from considering any other, wrapping itself around me in tenderness, giving me an impelling motive, having brought me to this conclusion, namely, that One died on behalf of all, therefore all died.*[3]

"One end"—one objective in life and no other, period. That is purity of heart. What kept Paul focused on that one objective? It was the love of Christ shown in His death for us. And what is the objective? To live no longer for ourselves but for Him who died for us.

Does this mean all other objectives are illegitimate? Not at all. We all have objectives. I have an objective to finish this book, another to do something special for my wife on our wedding anniversary, and on and on. But in all of these objectives we should keep in mind that the controlling objective of our lives is to live in continual awareness that Christ is the "owner" of our lives and that we are to live for Him, not for ourselves.

Another Scripture that is helpful in this discussion is Romans 12:1:

> *I appeal to you therefore, brothers, by the mercies of God, to present your bodies as a living sacrifice, holy and acceptable to God, which is your spiritual worship.*

To present our bodies (and our hearts also) is to recognize Christ as the "owner" of our lives. It is the subjective, experiential response to the objective truth that we are His own possession. But again, what does Paul present as the compelling motive to do this? It is the mercies of God as shown in the death of Christ in our place for our sins. (To pursue the extent of God's mercies further, see Romans 5:6-10 and Ephesians 2:1-7.)

It may seem as if I continually take us back to the gospel. That is true, for it is the love of Christ for us as seen in the gospel that provides both the right motive and the only enduring motivation to seek to be pure in heart.

But we need more than a proper motive and a lively motivation if we are to grow in purity of heart. We need the Holy Spirit to work in our hearts and to enable us to work. Two Scriptures sum up our responsibility to grow in purity of heart. The first is Psalm 86:11:

> *Teach me your way, O LORD,*
> *that I may walk in your truth;*
> *unite my heart to fear your name.*

We cannot by our own willpower unite our hearts to fear God—that is, to reverence Him and seek to glorify Him. That is why, like David, we should make prayer to this end a consistent part of our daily lives.

The second Scripture is Romans 12:2:

> *Do not be conformed to this world, but be transformed by*
> *the renewal of your mind, that by testing you may discern*
> *what is the will of God, what is good and acceptable and*
> *perfect.*

Though the Scriptures are not mentioned in that verse, they are clearly implied. Our minds can only be transformed as they are regularly exposed to the Word of God. This means we need to regularly read and study our Bibles and apply what we find there to our daily lives.

To be—or better, to seek to be—pure in heart produces humility in action as we become more God-focused in our daily lives. It requires humility to acknowledge that we no longer belong to ourselves but to Christ. And it is humbling to realize how much our hearts are divided—how often our desires, motives, emotions, and decision making are directed toward ourselves rather than Christ.

To acknowledge how far short we fall from purity of heart will send us back to the first Beatitudes: to be poor in spirit and to mourn because our hearts are so often divided. That is humbling. But that honest humility should drive us back to the gospel, where we see ourselves united to the One who had the only perfectly pure heart in all of history. This will motivate us and empower us to seek what we can never fully attain: to be pure in heart.

I love the old hymns I grew up with, and one I have recently been reflecting on is "My Faith Looks Up to Thee." The last phrases of the first stanza read as follows:

Take all my guilt away,
O let me from this day
Be wholly Thine!

Amen!

"Let me be wholly Thine." This is to be pure in heart. This is my prayer for myself, and I pray it is yours also.

CHAPTER EIGHT

PEACEMAKER

Blessed are the peacemakers,
for they shall be called sons of God.

MATTHEW 5:9

Conflict, and the resultant need for peacemaking, goes as far back in human history as Cain, son of Adam and Eve, who killed his brother Abel. Ever since then there has been conflict between tribes and nations, and in our own time between unions and management, students and school administrations—and, sad to say, too often between factions in churches or denominations, or even within families.

So today there is a great need for people who can play the role of peacemaker, whether between nations, between labor and management, or between students and administrations. There is even a fine organization called Peacemaker Ministries, which seeks to mediate peace within churches or families. We should be grateful for all the people who seek to be peacemakers at various levels of society.

But there is no doubt that Jesus did not have any of these

people in mind when He said, "Blessed are the peacemakers."
He was addressing His words to people who were powerless
to play the role of peacemaker on a national or international
scale. He did not even have in mind people who are gifted
and trained to bring peace within churches or families, as
important as that type of ministry is. Rather, as in all these
Beatitudes, He was speaking of something that should have
been true of all His listeners at that time, and should be true
of all believers today.

Jesus was speaking of making peace when we ourselves are
involved in conflict with others. So to explore this Beatitude,
we need to go to the root cause of conflict among ourselves.

As you read through the letters of the New Testament, you
will notice how often conflict is addressed. In Galatians 5:15
Paul warns, "But if you bite and devour one another, watch out
that you are not consumed by one another." When he writes
about the works of the flesh, along with flagrant sins such as immorality he mentions such sins as enmity, strife, jealousy, anger,
and the like (Galatians 5:19-21). When James asks, "What
causes quarrels and what causes fights among you?" (James
4:1), he is writing in the overall context of a discussion of the
razor-sharp tongue (James 3:6–4:2). In the Old Testament,
Solomon addresses the misuse of the tongue when he writes, "A
soft answer turns away wrath, but a harsh word stirs up anger"
(Proverbs 15:1).

It is often the sinful use of our tongues that causes conflict.
But the tongue is only an instrument. The real problem is the
heart, for Jesus said, "For out of the abundance of the heart the
mouth speaks" (Matthew 12:34). It is because of pride, anger,
jealousy, and the like in our hearts that we speak cutting and

hurtful words to one another. And it is because we nurse hurts from other people and harbor resentment in our hearts that we engage in verbal conflict.

To become peacemakers, then, we must begin with ourselves. We must ask ourselves, "Why do I make cutting remarks to another person? Why do I make demeaning remarks about them?" We must also ask ourselves, "What causes my resentment toward that person?" or "Why do I continue to nurse hurts by that person instead of forgiving them? What is it that causes me to be envious or jealous of that person?"

In order to even ask those questions, we have to admit that we have those attitudes. But because we know they are sinful, we tend to live in denial that we have them.

We need to deal with the sinful passions of our own hearts before we can deal with conflict of any kind with others. So where do we start? One way would be to go back over each of the character traits of the previous Beatitudes and to prayerfully and carefully ask ourselves how we compare with each of the traits. Am I poor in spirit? Do I mourn over my sin? Am I truly meek before God and with respect to other people? Do I truly hunger and thirst for righteousness, not only in my conduct but also in my heart? Am I merciful toward others who sin against me because I am aware of how merciful God has been to me? Do I seek a singleness of heart toward God based on the fact that I am no longer my own, but rather am Christ's possession? And if I am truly His possession, then does it really matter how I am treated? Because that is His business.

If we ask ourselves these questions with complete honesty, we should end up with a deep sense of humility. Only then are we in a position of becoming peacemakers.

Peacemaking where there is conflict with someone else is not an option for us. It is God's commandment. We are to *strive* for peace with everyone (Hebrews 12:14). The word *strive* is a translation of the Greek word *diōkō*. It is a very intense word and is most often used for the word *pursue*. Paul uses it in Philippians 3:12, 14 to say, "I press on." In 2 Timothy 2:22, he encourages Timothy to "pursue *[diōkō]* . . . peace." Peter, quoting from Psalm 34:14, writes, "let him seek peace and pursue *[diōkō]* it" (1 Peter 3:11). All these expressions convey an attitude of intensity, what I call a *sincere desire* and an *earnest effort* to bring about peace where there is conflict with another person. Paul's expression "I press on" seems to portray perseverance even in the face of a discouraging response from the other person or persons.

What might this look like in everyday life? Paul gives some admonitions in Romans 12:14-21.

Bless those who persecute you (verse 14) is an astounding statement: Instead of retaliating, we are to bless. We can easily pass by this instruction as not applying to us, because we do not suffer actual persecution. But there is a principle here that we should not ignore: We are to bless anyone who mistreats us in any way. Their mistreatment may be hurtful words or hurtful actions, but whatever they are, we are to bless the other person.

We certainly are not to *repay evil for evil* (verse 17), nor are we to *avenge ourselves* in any way (verse 19). Rather we are to leave vengeance to God. This does not mean that we pray for God's judgment on the person but rather that we entrust our situation to Him who judges with perfect justice.

We can easily see from the words of Jesus and from the writings of the apostle Paul, who wrote under the direct guidance of the Holy Spirit (2 Peter 1:21), that they turned the world's values upside down. To bless instead of retaliating, to leave justice in the hand of God instead of seeking it ourselves, is completely beyond society's values. And sadly, it often seems beyond our values. But if we are to live biblically, these are the standards we must seek to live by.

Despite our best efforts, however, there may be times when the person(s) we are in conflict with will not reciprocate. In that case, Paul says, "If possible, so far as it depends on you, live peaceably with all" (Romans 12:18). How can we do this? Jesus tells us, "Love your enemies and pray for those who persecute you" (Matthew 5:44). Are we willing to pray for those who have hurt us, that God will bless them?

To be a peacemaker, then, means we absorb the hurtful words or actions of others without becoming resentful, retaliating, or even cutting off a relationship with the person. When I mention hurtful actions, I do not include physically abusive actions. Addressing this issue is beyond the scope of this book, as the *process* of peacemaking. (In my opinion the best book to address the process is Ken Sande's *The Peacemaker*.[1]) But hurtful actions such as gossip, slander, or angry words addressed to someone can damage or even sever a relationship between two or more people. To be a peacemaker means taking the initiative to restore such broken or damaged relationships, even when the major cause of the rupture lies with the other person. And it especially requires taking the initiative when you are the one who has caused the damaged relationship.

To be a peacemaker means we must seek to be delivered from self-interest and not look at everything in terms of how it affects us. Instead we must be concerned about the glory of

God and how we can best promote that glory in situations of conflict. One of the greatest examples of humility in action is to act as a peacemaker in conflict that involves ourselves.

This humility cannot simply be worked up as an outward expression. It must come from the heart, and this is the work of the Holy Spirit. But the Holy Spirit uses means, and the chief means are God's Word and our prayers. So let me suggest two passages of Scripture in 1 Peter for you to ponder and pray over.

In 1 Peter 2:18-19 Peter addresses servants:

> *Servants, be subject to your masters with all respect, not only to the good and gentle but also to the unjust. For this is a gracious thing, when, mindful of God, one endures sorrows while suffering unjustly.*

Although he is addressing a specific situation, Peter is employing a principle that any of us can apply to any situation in which we are hurt or treated unjustly. Note Peter's words, "For this is a gracious thing, when, mindful of God, one endures sorrows while suffering unjustly," and again in verse 19, "this is a gracious thing in the sight of God." Why is it gracious in the sight of God? Because we are seeking to please and glorify Him instead of being concerned about ourselves.

Peter then invokes the example of Christ:

> *He committed no sin, neither was deceit found in his mouth.*
> *When he was reviled, he did not revile in return; when*
> *he suffered, he did not threaten, but continued entrusting*
> *himself to him who judges justly.*
>
> I PETER 2:22-23

Jesus' response when he was reviled answers the question, "What about the other person's sin? Who is going to deal with that?" Jesus entrusted the outcome to God, and so should we.

So if you are currently experiencing conflict, especially if you are the one hurt in the situation, I urge you to reflect on the principle in Peter's words to servants and then on the example of Jesus. Ponder these words carefully in the light of your situation, and ask the Holy Spirit to enable you by His power to apply them to your situation. In this way you will be displaying true humility in action.

Peacemaking can mean more than simply restoring a damaged relationship. It can also move beyond that to the development of a beautiful friendship. This is demonstrated in the experience of one of my best friends. Here is what he said:

A number of years ago in Michigan, my father died, and then a year later my mother died. I was married, had two children, and was living in California at the time. We all went back to Michigan for the funeral and to deal with the home and belongings of my folks.

I have one sister a few years older than me and had always had a difficult and troubled relationship with her. I generally felt rejected by her as a result of many hurtful events in our history. During the week after the funeral, the tension between us could not be denied. I actually thought that this could be the last time I would ever see her.

After returning to California I met with some close friends as part of a weekly time we had to share our lives and to grow together and with our Lord Jesus.

Upon hearing about my difficult time with my sister, one of the brothers said to me, "Do you love your sister?" I said, "Yes," and he asked, "How often are you in contact with her?" At that point I saw in my own heart that the only reason I ever connected with her was to do my duty and relieve me of any guilt. The fact was, I really didn't love her.

Shortly after that the Lord impressed on me His love for my sister and how important she was to Him. He also impressed on me that I needed to love her and that she was important to me.

Within a month or so I called her just to say hello and talk casually. I continued to do that every few months for a period of years. It was a long time before I ever received a call from her, but I was resolved to pursue her. I did it mechanically for a long time while God faithfully filled my cup with a genuine love for her.

After about four years she and her daughter came to visit my wife and me for a few days. We had a significant breakthrough. She told me that for the longest time she had wondered why I was calling her and then finally realized that I loved her.

Now as the years have passed, she and I are closer than I could ever have imagined. We love and respect each other. We talk often and cry and pray together over the phone. I can say that we are the *best* of friends. My sister, now a widow, loves me and calls me the favorite man in her life, and I love her dearly.

That is an example of what it means to be a peacemaker.

CHAPTER NINE

PERSECUTED FOR RIGHTEOUSNESS' SAKE

Blessed are those who are persecuted for
righteousness' sake, for theirs is the kingdom of heaven.
Blessed are you when others revile you and persecute you
and utter all kinds of evil against you falsely on my account.
Rejoice and be glad, for your reward is great in heaven,
for so they persecuted the prophets who were before you.

MATTHEW 5:10-12

Persecution of God's people is as old as the history of humanity. Reading through the Old Testament would confirm this, but the persecution of those times is best summarized by the writer of Hebrews:

Some were tortured, refusing to accept release, so that they
might rise again to a better life. Others suffered mocking
and flogging, and even chains and imprisonment. They
were stoned, they were sawn in two, they were killed with
the sword. They went about in skins of sheep and goats,
destitute, afflicted, mistreated.

HEBREWS 11:35-37

Persecution continued into the New Testament era, with Stephen as the first Christian martyr (see Acts 7). The apostle Paul, before his conversion when he was called Saul of Tarsus, "persecuted the church" (1 Corinthians 15:9). In every century since then, people have been persecuted for Christ's sake, sometimes even by unbelieving religious authorities. Yet it is a commonly recognized fact that there were more Christian martyrs in the twentieth century than any preceding one, and this is continuing in the twenty-first century. Persecution of believers is very real in some parts of the world today.

It is difficult for those of us living in the Western world to identify with this fact of relentless persecution of Christians. In fact I find it challenging to even address this eighth Beatitude because I have not personally experienced persecution of any form for my faith, nor do I know anyone who has.

But the reality is that many people are facing nonphysical persecution because of their stand for righteousness. This nonphysical persecution may come in different forms. It may be political, economic, or social persecution. It may be job discrimination or even dismissal. It may be denial of tenure to a university professor who does not hold to "politically correct" views on various social issues. Now there is a growing movement among public universities to require religious student groups to admit anyone to membership or even leadership, regardless of their faith or lack of it. This requirement seems to be particularly targeted toward Christian organizations.

I predict the various types of nonphysical persecution will become more widespread and intense. There is an old adage that says if you put a frog into a kettle of boiling water, it will leap out immediately to escape the danger. However, if you put that same frog into water with a pleasant temperature, and then gradually increase the heat until it starts boiling, the frog will not become aware of the threat until it's too late. I think the "kettle" of our culture has been heating up for some time and will soon reach the boiling stage. So we need to be prepared to respond in ways that honor God.

There is no doubt that the culture is becoming more and more antagonistic toward biblical values. For some years I have thought of our American culture to be ungodly; that is, to believe and act as if God is irrelevant. Now I believe we have become not just ungodly but actually anti-God. An increasing number of those who most influence our culture—such as academia, the media, and the entertainment industry—are openly hostile to the whole idea of God or of biblical values. So how are we to respond?

It is true that in America we have a court system and the First Amendment protection of the free exercise of religion that we can resort to, and we should use that when necessary to defend our religious freedom. After all, the apostle Paul twice claimed his Roman citizenship as protection against unlawful persecution (see Acts 16:35-39; 22:22-29). And when he realized that the Roman legal system in Caesarea was biased against him, he appealed directly to Caesar (Acts 25:11)—even though Caesar eventually failed him (2 Timothy 4:6).

I suspect that our own court system will eventually fail us, as more and more judges are appointed who have been trained in law schools that at best are indifferent to biblical righteousness and at worst are openly hostile to it. Even our Supreme Court seems to be rendering decisions based on the mores of popular culture rather than on a principled application of the Constitution.

It is quite apparent that the Bible no longer has moral authority in society as a whole. So we should expect increasing marginalization of Christians, and in some instances curtail-ment of our religious freedom. How should we respond? Certainly not in a combative cultural-warfare attitude. Rather, it should be based on the principle Jesus taught in Matthew 5:44: "But I say to you, Love your enemies and pray for those who persecute you."

As I observe the response of so many Christians to the erod-ing of what have been called "traditional values," I am con-cerned that we are acting no differently than many nonbelievers who may care nothing about the Bible but who want to defend those values. Instead of loving those whose actions and lifestyles we oppose, we seem to engage in some form of action that is inconsistent with Jesus' admonition to love our enemies.

In the mid-1970s, abortion was hotly protested by Christians, and rightfully so. I attended a meeting on the subject of the proper Christian response, and I remember a Christian leader saying that we evangelicals should become cobelligerents with Catholics, who also staunchly opposed abortion. Technically the word *cobelligerent* means a country fighting with another power against a common enemy. The speaker was adapting it to the abortion topic. I suspect we all agreed with him at the time, but as I reflect back on that meeting, I am appalled that he used (and we accepted) the term *cobelligerent*. Allies, yes, but cobelligerents? The term denotes hostility. It certainly does not suggest the humility that Christ taught when He called on us to love our enemies and pray for those who persecute us.

There is a sense in which this eighth Beatitude is the cli-max of several preceding ones dealing with our response to the way others treat us. In the third Beatitude, Jesus teaches us to practice meekness toward those who mistreat us in any way.

In the fifth Beatitude we are taught to forgive others, however much they may sin against us. And the seventh Beatitude teaches us to strive for peace with all people, regardless of who is at fault. The "others" in these Beatitudes may or may not be fellow believers—though, sad to say, they often are. But in this eighth Beatitude Jesus has in mind persecution rooted in the hostility of the anti-God culture we live in.

Surprisingly, in this Beatitude Jesus does not address our response to those who persecute us. But as I have already mentioned, He does so elsewhere in the Sermon on the Mount. In Matthew 5:44, He says, "Love your enemies and pray for those who persecute you." In Luke's account of this sermon, Jesus says, "But I say to you who hear, Love your enemies, do good to those who hate you, bless those who curse you, pray for those who abuse you" (Luke 6:27-28). Keep in mind these words from Jesus are *precepts*—authoritative commands of God. Furthermore, they address more than our *attitude* toward those who persecute us. They are *action* steps: We are to *love* our enemies, *do good* to them, *bless* them, and *pray* for them. Specifically what these action steps will be will vary according to different situations, but they should be governed by these words from Jesus, and by the realization that these people have eternal souls and will spend eternity either in heaven or hell.

Another important question is, How will we respond if our religious freedom is curtailed and our court protection fails us? Will we consider ourselves to be blessed because of being reviled or persecuted for righteousness' sake? When push comes to shove, will we really believe that God is sovereign over all the affairs of humanity? Will we believe the words that King Nebuchadnezzar learned by experience?

All the inhabitants of the earth are accounted as nothing,
and he does according to his will among the host of heaven
and among the inhabitants of the earth;
and none can stay his hand
or say to him, "What have you done?"

DANIEL 4:35

Will we believe that, despite many appearances to the contrary, Jesus is building His church and "the gates of hell shall not prevail against it" (Matthew 16:18)?

I put all these statements in the form of questions because I do not know if I myself would answer them correctly, and act accordingly, if and when the difficult day comes. But I believe that the day is coming and that we should begin now to prepare for how to respond in a God-honoring way.

As we consider our Christian response to persecution, we should also think carefully about our response to governmental authorities. Our best scriptural guidance on this subject is probably 1 Peter 2:13-17:

Be subject for the Lord's sake to every human institution,
whether it be to the emperor as supreme, or to governors as
sent by him to punish those who do evil and to praise those
who do good. For this is the will of God, that by doing good
you should put to silence the ignorance of foolish people. Live
as people who are free, not using your freedom as a cover-up
for evil, but living as servants of God. Honor everyone. Love
the brotherhood. Fear God. Honor the emperor.

Peter wrote those words during the reign of Nero, one of the most terrible persecutors of Christians, and he says, "Honor the emperor." Remember, Peter wrote under the divine guidance of the Holy Spirit, so this is another precept from God. We are to honor those in authority over us (see also Romans 13:1-7).

It is difficult in our democratic society—where we elect our governing authorities all the way from president to county commissioners—to know how to apply Peter's directives, which were given in the context of the absolute rule of the emperor and his appointed local rulers.

I believe the key word is *honor*, or we might say *respect*. Even when we totally disagree with an elected official, we should respect the office.

But in our democratic and increasingly egalitarian society we have largely lost the concept of respect. Twelve presidents have served our country during my adult life. I have often disagreed with some of their policies and actions. But I believe the Bible teaches me to honor and respect them because God, acting through our electoral process, has sovereignly installed them in that office. As Daniel said, "The Most High rules the kingdom of men and gives it to whom he will" (Daniel 4:25). So a biblical response toward those who might persecute us, and a biblical attitude toward governing authorities over us, are both expressions of humility in action.

Meanwhile, as we struggle to act biblically in our increasingly anti-God society, let us consider our brothers and sisters in Christ who are suffering real persecution (and sometimes even death) in many countries of the world today. Even though Jesus said they are blessed (Matthew 5:10-12), persecution makes their lives difficult and painful. We should be praying regularly for God's sustaining grace for them, as well as for safety and deliverance from their persecutors. We may think prayer for our persecuted brothers and sisters is a meager or even useless effort, but remember the words of James: "The prayer of a righteous person has great power as it is working" (James 5:16). God is still on His throne, and as Proverbs 21:1 says, "The king's heart is a stream of water in the hands of the LORD; he turns it wherever he will."

We will gain a true perspective of our own suffering when we realize how much more our persecuted brothers and sisters are going through.

As I have been working on this chapter, one verse of an old hymn by the great English hymn writer Isaac Watts (1674–1748) kept coming to my mind. I include this stanza of "Am I a Soldier of the Cross" here, praying that it will challenge you as much as it has challenged me.

> *Must I be carried to the skies*
> *On flowery beds of ease,*
> *While others fought to win the prize,*
> *And sailed through bloody seas?*

In God's providence, those of us in the West are, for the most part, experiencing the "flowery beds of ease." May we consistently and prayerfully remember those in other parts of the world who are "sail[ing] through bloody seas." This will be another demonstration of humility in action.

CHAPTER TEN

HUMILITY AND THE GOSPEL

*And Jesus answered them, "Those who are
well have no need of a physician, but those
who are sick. I have not come to call the
righteous but sinners to repentance."*

LUKE 5:31-32

The apostle Paul wrote his first letter to the Corinthians about AD 54. In it he referred to himself as the "least of the apostles" (1 Corinthians 15:9). In AD 62, in his letter to the Ephesians, he considered himself as the "very least of all the saints" (that is, all believers—Ephesians 3:8). In about AD 63–64, in his first letter to Timothy, he referred to himself as the foremost of sinners (1 Timothy 1:15).

From the least of the apostles, to the very least of all the saints, to the foremost of sinners, all in the space of about ten years. On the surface it seemed as if Paul was regressing in his Christian life, but in actuality he was progressing. Paul was growing in humility, one of the two most basic character traits of a Christian (the other being love).

If you have honestly evaluated yourself in the light of the eight character traits in the Beatitudes, you have probably seen yourself to be a worse sinner than you thought. You might even want to join the apostle Paul as the foremost of sinners. If that is your self-evaluation, you are in a good place. That is a sign that you also are growing in humility. What is it, though, that will keep us from becoming discouraged as we become more and more aware of the sin that still dwells within us? The answer is the gospel.

It is in the gospel, the Good News, that our sins—however many there may be, and however ugly they are—have all been forgiven through Christ's death on the cross. And furthermore, not only are we forgiven, but we also are actually credited with the righteousness of Christ Himself.

Most Christians assume that the gospel is only for unbelievers. They see the gospel only as a door you walk through to be saved. The reality, though, is that the gospel is more like a path that you walk along for the rest of your life until you go to be with the Lord. To put it in plain words, believers need to appropriate the gospel for themselves every day. Why? Because we are still practicing sinners every day, and without the daily assurance of the gospel, we can begin to think that, at least for that day, we have lost the favor of God.

Some people who genuinely want to grow in Christian character say that it seems as if "God keeps moving the goalposts": The more they grow, the more they see they need to grow.

The truth is, however, that God does not keep moving the goalposts. He has established one unmovable goalpost that none of us can ever reach. That goal is stated in Galatians 3:10:

> For all who rely on works of the law are under a curse; for it is written, "Cursed be everyone who does not abide by all things written in the Book of the Law, and do them."

Note the phrase "all things." In context, *all* is an absolute term. It means "without exception."

The "all things" of Galatians 3:10 refers to the "Book of the Law." Someone has counted that there are over six hundred laws from God just in the Old Testament. But Jesus summed them all up in just two:

> *You shall love the Lord your God with all your heart and with all your soul and with all your mind. This is the great and first commandment. And a second is like it: You shall love your neighbor as yourself. On these two commandments depend all the Law and the Prophets.*
>
> MATTHEW 22:37-40

Jesus summed up all those six-hundred-plus commandments in just two: Love God supremely, and love your neighbor as yourself. That is God's unmovable goalpost. And none of us has even come close to reaching it, even on our very best days.

That is the bad news. But the good news is that there is One who did reach it: our Lord Jesus Christ.

During Jesus' thirty-three years on earth, He lived a perfectly righteous life. He never once sinned. The New Testament writers consistently testify to Christ's sinlessness. Paul said He "knew no sin" (2 Corinthians 5:21). The writer of Hebrews said, "In every respect [He] has been tempted as we are, yet without sin" (Hebrews 4:15). The apostle Peter wrote, "He committed no sin" (1 Peter 2:22), and John said, "In him there is no sin" (1 John 3:5). Jesus Himself said, "I always do the things that are pleasing to [the Father]" (John 8:29).

Yes, Jesus reached the goalpost of perfect righteousness. In fact, we shouldn't say He *reached* it; rather He was always there, from the moment of His birth until the moment He gave up His life on the cross. Thirty-three years of perfect righteousness, and He lived it all in our place as our representative before God. At the end of that perfectly righteous life, He willingly died on the cross to satisfy the justice of God, again in our place and as our substitute before God.

The first chapter in this book is titled "Precepts and Promises," but there is another word association that is equally valid: "precepts and penalties." Every law, even in our temporal realm, has to have a penalty attached to it; otherwise, it is unenforceable. And with God's law, the penalty is death—both physical death and eternal, spiritual death (Romans 6:23). Jesus both perfectly obeyed God's law and then paid the penalty for our failure to perfectly obey it. We return to the beautiful observation that "he lived a life we could not live and died the death we deserved to die."

This is the gospel, the message of "good news." This is the door each of us must walk through by trusting in Christ as the One who bore *our* sins in His body on the cross. But as I said earlier, the gospel is also a path we must walk along until the day we die. As I walk along, I learn that Jesus not only died in my place, but He also lived that perfectly righteous life in my place. That's when the good news of the gospel really becomes good news!

How, then, does this good news of the gospel help us live our daily lives in humility? For one thing, it frees us up to be honest with ourselves about our sin. We can face our sin squarely when we know that it is forgiven. Even when a particular sin is vile in our eyes—not to mention God's eyes—we can call it what it is, and thank God for His forgiveness.

My personal way of doing this is to acknowledge the particular sin without any excuses, and then quote Isaiah 53:6 to myself and to God: "All we like sheep have gone astray; we have turned—every one—to his own way." I stop at that point and say, "Lord, that's me in this sin. I've turned to my own way." And then I continue, "And You, Lord have laid on Him, Your Son, all of my iniquity—even this ugly sin I am now confessing." I do this, or something similar, as I become aware of sin throughout the day.

The second way the gospel helps us live a life of humility is to show us another person's sin in the light of our own. To paraphrase and even enlarge on the words of one of the Puritans, the proud (or self-righteous) person is so busy judging the sins of other people that he or she has no time to see the sins of his or her own heart. Meanwhile, the humble person is so busy dealing with his or her own sins that he or she has no time to judge the sins of others.

Many people, when presented with another person's sin, repeat the cliché "There but for the grace of God go I." Often they use the phrase unthinkingly; even worse, sometimes the phrase is used to subtly say, "I would never do that," or to subtly put down someone who has spoken disparagingly of another person. So instead of being an expression of genuine humility, it can become an expression of self-righteous pride. Such is the deceitfulness of our renewed but still-sinful hearts. But when spoken or even thought sincerely, this is a good expression that should promote humility.

A third way the gospel helps us walk in humility is that it helps us practice meekness and mercy (see chapters 4 and 6). We can only truly appreciate the gospel when we see it through the lens of our own sin. And as we do that, we can forgive the sins of others because we have been forgiven so much.

Fourth, the gospel motivates us to want to live in purity of heart—that is, to have as our supreme goal in life to live no longer for ourselves but for Him who redeemed us to be a people for His own possession. Recall from chapter 7 that it was the love of Christ for Paul, as seen in the death of Christ, that constrained him to live that way. As I mentioned in chapter 7, I find myself often praying over a few phrases from the old hymn "My Faith Looks Up to Thee."

Take all my guilt away,
O let me from this day
Be wholly Thine!

"Take all my guilt away"—that is clinging to the gospel. "O let me from this day be wholly Thine"—that is prayer for purity of heart. But that desire is fueled by the gospel.

In summary, I would say that it is impossible to truly walk in humility without to some degree appropriating the truth of the gospel every day. The natural question then is, how does one do this? It is by developing a practice of meditating on and praying over key Scriptures on the gospel. They have to be of your own choosing—verses that speak powerfully to you. But to give you a place to begin, the following are Scriptures that I choose from for daily appropriation of the gospel.

My all-time favorite Scripture on the gospel is 2 Corinthians 5:21: "For our sake he made him to be sin who knew no sin, so that in him we might become the righteousness of God." This verse needs some explanation, however, to help us understand what Paul is saying. God making Christ "to be sin" does not mean that He made Him to be a sinner but that He made Him to *bear* our sin. God the Father took *all* the sin of *all* of us—sins of commission and omission; sins in thought, word, deed, and motive; sins we are not even aware of; *all* of them—and laid them on the head of His beloved Son. He charged the *entire* debt of *all* our sins to Christ. And through His death on the cross, Christ paid the debt.

The Scripture that helps me best understand Paul's meaning is Isaiah 53:6:

> *All we like sheep have gone astray;*
> *we have turned—every one—to his own way;*
> *and the LORD has laid on him*
> *the iniquity of us all.*

Note the latter part of the verse: "The LORD has laid on him the iniquity of us all." That's what Paul meant when he wrote, "[God] made him to be sin."

You might want to also memorize the preceding verse, Isaiah 53:5, for reflection:

> *But he was pierced for our transgressions;*
> *he was crushed for our iniquities;*
> *upon him was the chastisement that brought us peace,*
> *and with his wounds we are healed.*

That Scripture fleshes out in more detail the meaning of verse 6.

To make the truth of verse 5 more personal, I like to change the pronouns. The verse would then read,

> *You were pierced for my transgressions;*
> *You were crushed for my iniquities;*

> *upon You was the chastisement that brought me peace,*
>   *and with Your wounds I am healed.*

In that way I really do appropriate the gospel for myself—or, to use a now well-known expression, "I preach the gospel to myself every day."

The latter part of 2 Corinthians 5:21—"so that in him we might become the righteousness of God"—also needs some explaining. We obviously do not become in ourselves as righteous as God Himself. The key to understanding Paul's words are two little words: *in him.* This is Paul's shorthand expression for our representative union with Christ. God appointed Jesus to be the representative before Him of all who trust in Jesus for our salvation. So all that Christ did in His sinless life and sin-bearing death, He did in our place as our representative. So the expression "in him we might become the righteousness of God" means that we might be counted as righteous by God *because* He credits to us the perfect righteousness that Jesus lived out over thirty-three years.

The Scripture that helps me most to understand and apply what Paul is saying is Philippians 3:9:

> . . . *and be found in him, not having a righteousness of my own that comes from the law, but that which comes through faith in Christ, the righteousness from God that depends on faith.*

The context of this verse is Paul's personal testimony of how he totally renounced any confidence in his own law-keeping righteousness in order to rely totally on Christ's righteousness. Note that he speaks of "the righteousness *from* God that depends on faith." Again Paul uses his shorthand expression, "in him," to indicate that it is through his representative union with Christ that he receives this righteousness from God—or, to say it another way, God credits the righteousness of Christ to him.

So 2 Corinthians 5:21, Isaiah 53:6 (and sometimes verse 5), and Philippians 3:9 are my primary verses for daily appropriating the gospel. I sometimes also use some of the following verses:

"As far as the east is from the west, so far does he remove our transgressions from us" (Psalm 103:12). "As far as the east is from the west" is an idiom meaning an infinite distance. Someone has pointed out that, although north and south meet at the two poles, east and west never meet. You can start flying north, to the North Pole, and as soon as you pass over it, you are immediately heading south. But if you start west to circle the earth you will always be flying west. East never meets west. So to use the expression "as far as the east is from the west" means that my sins are completely wiped away. God has put them out of His mind. He remembers them no more (see Hebrews 8:12; 10:17).

"Though your sins are like scarlet, they shall be as white as snow; though they are red like crimson, they shall become like wool" (Isaiah 1:18). This is the Scripture I go to when I feel particularly guilty of my sin. Scarlet is one of the most difficult dyes to remove from clothing. In this verse God is saying that, no matter how deep the guilt of our sin is, He will completely remove it. In the New Testament we learn that He does this through the death of Christ.

"I, I am he who blots out your transgressions for my own sake, and I will not remember your sins" (Isaiah 43:25). To blot out transgressions means to remove them from God's record book.

It is in a sense a legal transaction. To remember them no more is a relational act.

"You will cast all our sins into the depths of the sea" (Micah 7:19). I love this Scripture because, as a former navy man, I know what it means for something to be cast into the depths of the sea. It is gone forever. This is a vivid picture of what God does with our sins.

"Blessed are those whose lawless deeds are forgiven, and whose sins are covered; blessed is the man against whom the Lord will not count his sin" (Romans 4:7-8). I especially like verse 8, which says the Lord will not count our sins against us. He will not do this because He has already counted our sins against His own Son. In considering the truth of God's forgiveness, we must never think that God simply writes off our debt of sin, or, so to speak, sweeps it under some cosmic rug. No, the debt must be paid. God's justice must be satisfied. But the good news of the gospel is that Jesus paid the debt in full. He satisfied God's justice completely. It is on that basis that God no longer counts our sin against us.

"There is therefore now no condemnation for those who are in Christ Jesus" (Romans 8:1). This is a good verse to go to when we feel condemned. We feel condemned because we know we are guilty. God knows that, too, but He doesn't condemn us because He has already dealt with that sin through Christ.

"For, being ignorant of the righteousness of God, and seeking to establish their own, they did not submit to God's righteousness. For Christ is the end of the law for righteousness to everyone who believes" (Romans 10:3-4). This is a good passage of Scripture to go along with Philippians 3:9 regarding the righteousness of Christ that is credited to us. Note that Christ is the end

of the law for righteousness. He is the end of the law for us because He perfectly fulfilled it as our representative. We now stand righteous before God on that basis. Christ is not the end of the law as far as its moral precepts are concerned. Those are still valid for us as an expressions of God's moral will, by which we seek by obedience to please Him and glorify Him.

These are the Scriptures I use to daily appropriate the gospel. In addition to my primary ones (2 Corinthians 5:21; Isaiah 53:6; Philippians 3:9), I will choose one or two others that, for some reason, are especially meaningful to me that day.

One final thought, however, about preaching the gospel (or appropriating it) to yourself. In the Scripture at the beginning of this chapter Jesus said, "Those who are well have no need of a physician, but those who are sick. I have not come to call the righteous but sinners to repentance" (Luke 5:31-32). The gospel is only for sinners, so we must come to the gospel as still-practicing sinners with an attitude of repentance toward our sin. Our sin may be only what I call "respectable" sins in our eyes, but all sin is vile in the eyes of our infinitely holy God. So we must come with the humility of the tax collector praying in the temple: "God be merciful to me, *the* sinner."

As we have gone through the Beatitudes, we have found that the truly humble person

- is poor in spirit,
- mourns over his or her sin,
- is meek toward God and other people,
- hungers and thirsts for righteousness,
- is merciful toward other people,
- is pure in heart,

- is a peacemaker, and
- considers himself or herself blessed when persecuted or reviled for righteousness' sake.

This is a formidable list, one that none of us will ever perfectly attain to. That is why we need the gospel every day. It is the gospel that will keep us from becoming discouraged and will instead motivate us to keep pursuing humility, even when we fail so often.

We also need to daily realize our dependence on the work and power of the Holy Spirit to pursue the various expressions of humility. There is a fundamental principle of spiritual growth that I call "the principle of dependent responsibility." For example, God says through Paul, "Walk in . . . humility." We are responsible for doing that, but we must depend on the Holy Spirit to enable us. Furthermore, we are dependent on the Holy Spirit to work genuine change in our hearts. As Paul said, "[It is] only God who gives the growth" (1 Corinthians 3:7).

This principle is taught in various ways throughout the Bible, but is concisely stated in the words of Hebrews 13:21: "[May God] equip you with everything good that you may do his will." Here the emphasis is on what we do. For example, *we* walk in humility, but only with His equipping or enabling power. The verse then continues: ". . . working in us that which is pleasing in his sight." This refers to the mysterious work of the Holy Spirit in our inner being as He transforms us more and more into the image of Christ. Both of these works of the Spirit are necessary.

As we grow in the Christian life, then, we become increasingly aware of our dependence on the righteousness of Christ revealed to us through the gospel. And we also become increasingly aware of our dependence on the Holy Spirit. Both of these awarenesses are expressions of humility. In our dependence on the righteousness that is in Christ and on the power of the Holy Spirit, may we all seek to grow in humility as we see it in the eight character traits of the Beatitudes.

DISCUSSION GUIDE

CHAPTER ONE

1. When Paul describes what it means to walk worthy of our calling, he lists *humility* first. Why do you think God's Word puts humility before *gentleness*, *patience*, and *love*?

2. Why is a life of humility not an option for a believer to choose or reject?

3. In what ways did Jesus Christ display humility? Why are these examples so astonishing?

4. Which of the precepts described in this chapter do you find most challenging? Which of the promises do you find most motivating?

CHAPTER TWO

1. How has this chapter changed your understanding of what it means to be *poor* in spirit? How has it changed your understanding of what it means to be poor in *spirit*?

2. How can a Christian who is growing spiritually and becoming more like Christ be poor in spirit at the same time?

3. In moments when you see yourself as truly poor in spirit, where should your attention turn next?

4. How do those who are poor in spirit view others? themselves? God's Word? their circumstances?

CHAPTER THREE

1. How is "mourning over your sin" different from *regret*, *sorrow*, or even *shedding tears* over your sin?

2. When was the last time you truly mourned over your sin?
   What impact did the process have on your self-image? your
   relationships with others? your relationship with God?

3. James 2:10 says, "For whoever keeps the whole law but
   fails in one point has become accountable for all of
   it." From God's perspective, why is this a simple truth?
   How should you respond when you become aware of the
   "smallest" sin?

4. How can mourning over your sin serve as an antidote
   for pride?

CHAPTER FOUR

1. Have you desired the character quality of meekness?
   Why or why not?

2. Explain how the character traits of the first three
   Beatitudes build on one another. Why is meekness an

inevitable outflow from poverty in spirit and mourning over our sin?

3. Look at Romans 8:28 in the context of Romans 8:29. What is the definition of *good*? Why is understanding this a key to developing biblical meekness?

4. What basis does God's Word provide for forgiving those who appear to be unforgivable?

CHAPTER FIVE

1. What is the biblical definition of *righteousness*? What evidence is there in the Bible to show that Jesus Christ met the requirements of this definition?

2. Why is Christ's sinless life equally important as His sacrificial death for our sin?

3. What does the author mean by the expression "positional righteousness"? If you are in Christ, how does this make you feel inside?

4. What does the author mean by the expression "experiential righteousness"? What evidence is there in the Bible to prove that you should actively pursue it?

5. What motivates the genuine Christian to pursue experiential righteousness?

CHAPTER SIX

1. Explain the differences between showing *pity* toward someone and showing them *mercy*.

2. What did it *cost* God to be merciful toward us by forgiving our sins?

3. "To forgive others means we regard ourselves as ten-thousand-talent debtors." What does the author mean by this statement?

4. Think back to the last time you were merciful to someone who wronged you. What did it cost you to be able to say, "You don't owe me anymore"?

CHAPTER SEVEN

1. Jesus said, "Blessed are the pure in heart." What did He mean by *pure*? What did He mean by *heart*?

2. How would you evaluate the purity of your heart, on a scale of 1 to 10, in light of this chapter?

3. Why is the first car illustration an insufficient way to explain the lordship of Christ?

4. What is the most powerful motivation for surrendering
   to the fact that you do not own yourself, but Christ does?

5. As you seek to be pure in heart, what is the vital role
   of the Holy Spirit? the Scriptures?

CHAPTER EIGHT

1. The author states, "To become peacemakers . . . we must
   begin with ourselves." Why is this true?

2. How can applying each of the previous six Beatitudes
   be instrumental in setting you up to become a
   peacemaker?

3. How can Peter's words to servants in 1 Peter 2:18-20
   and the example of Jesus in 1 Peter 2:22-23 make all the
   difference when someone wrongs you?

4. What evidence in the Bible shows that sins in the area of interpersonal relationships are as important as sins in the area of sexuality and integrity? In light of this, what actions should you take?

CHAPTER NINE

1. In what ways have you experienced persecution for your faith in Christ?

2. Do you agree with the author's view that America has become not just ungodly but actually anti-God? Why or why not?

3. What difference should the command of Jesus in Matthew 5:44 make when you, as a Christian, consider your response to political or legislated opposition to biblical morality?

4. What are we to learn and apply from 1 Peter 2:13-17 and Romans 13:1-7, and especially the biblical mandate

to "honor the emperor"? Do you believe the Christian mainstream is doing this today? Why or why not?

5. How is seeing persecution as a blessing a tangible way of displaying humility in action?

CHAPTER TEN

1. Take some time to honestly evaluate yourself in the light of the eight character traits in the Beatitudes. Do you see yourself to be a worse sinner than you thought? Why or why not?

2. Name some specific ways in which the gospel alone can keep you from becoming discouraged as you develop humility in action by applying the Beatitudes.

3. What is the one simple reason why you need to appropriate the gospel for yourself every day?

4. What are four ways in which the good news of the gospel helps you live your daily life in humility?

5. What Bible verses or passages will you use to begin to develop a lifelong practice of meditating on and praying over key Scriptures on the gospel?

NOTES

CHAPTER 2: POOR IN SPIRIT
1. John Blanchard, *Right with God* (Edinburgh: Banner of Truth, 1971), 86.

CHAPTER 3: MOURN
1. Blanchard, *Right with God,* 97.

CHAPTER 4: MEEK
1. Thomas Watson, *The Beatitudes* (Edinburgh: Banner of Truth, 1971), 106.
2. Blanchard, *Right with God,* 133.

CHAPTER 7: PURE IN HEART
1. Blanchard, *Right with God,* 189–90.
2. Mabel Williamson, *Have We No Rights?* (Chicago: Moody Press, 1957).
3. 2 Corinthians 5:14-15, in Kenneth S. Wuest, *The New Testament: An Expanded Translation* (Grand Rapids, MI: Eerdmans, 1961).

CHAPTER 8: PEACEMAKER
1. Ken Sande, *The Peacemaker: A Biblical Guide to Resolving Personal Conflict,* third edition (Grand Rapids, MI: Baker Books, 2004).

AUTHOR

 JERRY BRIDGES was a well-known Christian writer and conference speaker. His best-known book, *The Pursuit of Holiness*, has sold well over a million copies. A prolific author, he sold over 3.5 million copies of his various books, with several titles translated and published in a variety of foreign languages. He joined the staff of The Navigators in 1955, serving for sixty years as a staff member in various capacities before transitioning to an associate staff position and serving within the collegiate ministry. Jerry passed away in the spring of 2016, leaving behind his wife, Jane; two married children; and seven grandchildren.

JERRY BRIDGES

GOD TOOK ME
by the HAND

A Story of God's
UNUSUAL PROVIDENCE

GOD TOOK ME BY THE HAND

by Jerry Bridges

Publisher's note: In 2014 Jerry Bridges published a memoir that demonstrates both the principle that "the Bible is meant to be applied in your everyday life"—that comment from January 1952 that was so life-changing for him—and the concept of "humility in action" articulated throughout this book. Included here is an excerpt from *God Took Me by the Hand*, as a window into how God's providence has operated in Jerry's life and an encouragement to consider how your own story might reflect the humility in action that characterizes a normal Christian life.

AN UNPROMISING
BEGINNING

The 500 block of Oakland Avenue ran parallel to and about ten yards west of the railroad tracks. Those ten yards between the tracks and the street were owned by the railroad company and sat empty most of the time. The one exception was when the railroad used that empty land to store rail ties.

Across the unpaved road, alone in the middle of the block, sat a small four-room house, 521 South Oakland Avenue. I do not know the origin of the house, but it quite possibly had been servants' quarters for the larger house on the other side of the block. Whatever its origin, the house was very plain. There were no closets. Clothes were hung on hooks on the walls. There were no kitchen cabinets. The house did have indoor plumbing, but there was no hot water heater. In order to wash clothes or the dishes or to take a bath, one had to heat water on the kitchen stove and mix it with cold water from the faucets. I was born in this house on December 4, 1929. My parents named me Gerald Dean but called me Jerry, and that is the name I have gone by all my life, except in legal and financial documents.

My parents were Emmett and Lillian Bridges. Both had grown up on East Texas cotton farms, and both had dropped out of school after eighth grade to work on the farms. They were married about 1924, and Dad started raising cotton on rented land. Their first child was born June 4, 1926, and was named William Jackson but was called Jack. Sometime after Jack was born, my dad realized he could never succeed raising cotton on rented land, so he sold what little assets he had and moved the family to Tyler, Texas, a town of about twenty thousand people. His plan was to go to a business college and study accounting. However, he got sidetracked.

He took a job with a farm supply store which also had a cotton brokerage business. The owners of the company talked him into studying cotton grading so he could become their cotton buyer. The problem was that buying cotton was seasonal, and Dad spent the rest of the year as a clerk in the farm supply store. Humanly speaking, this was not a good decision. Though Dad had dropped out of school after eighth grade, he was very intelligent and was especially good at math. I'm sure he would have made an excellent basic accountant. However, viewed from the perspective I now have, I am confident that God was sovereignly directing that seemingly bad decision. God is as much in control of our bad decisions as He is our good ones. This does not mean God *causes* us to make bad decisions any more than He causes us to sin. But He does allow us to sin, and He does allow us to make our bad decisions.

When I was born I had four physical defects. The first and

most obvious was that I was cross-eyed. For those not familiar with this term, it means that while one eye looks straight ahead the other eye is turned toward the nose. The second and most difficult to deal with is that my right inner ear was not fully developed. As a young child I was not aware of my deafness in that ear, but I became increasingly aware of it and the accompanying inconvenience as I grew older. It was not until I was eighty-two that an ear, nose, and throat doctor discovered the cause of my deafness which I had had all my life.

The third and fourth defects were deformities in my breastbone and spine. Actually, these two were not significant in my growing up years, but both became quite a problem in adult life. Then to add insult to injury, I became left-handed in a right-handed world. I did not get off to a good start physically.

My parents were members of a "fundamentalist" church. That word did not have the derogatory ring in those days that it has now. Nevertheless, it was a small, separatist church. My mother was a homebody who never learned to drive and didn't socialize much in the neighborhood. In fact, her whole social life took place in the church. Dad worked from 8 a.m. to 6 p.m. six days a week. With church activities on Sunday, he had no time for neighborhood socializing.

To sum it up, my parents were financially poor, education dropouts, and religiously and socially isolated. This was not a good beginning for me.

My brother, Jack, started school when I was only two years old, and there were no boys my age in the neighborhood, so I grew up alone until I started school at age six. We had no toys, so I played in my imagination. My favorite was pretending to be an over-the-road truck driver complete with all the sounds of engines revving up and gears meshing, which I heard in the real trucks in my neighborhood.

Finally the day came in 1936 for me to start school. Our school system did not have a kindergarten grade at that time, so I started in first grade. Again, because my mother was a home-body, instead of taking me to school the first day, she sent me with my brother, Jack, who was entering fifth grade. All was well until we got to the school, and then Jack did not know what to do with me. He was so bewildered he started to cry and the principal came along, asked his problem, and got me safely to my first-grade class.

Years later, as I thought back on my early childhood from the advantage of knowing what I had learned about the providence of God, two verses of Scripture helped. They are Psalm 139:13 and 16: "For you formed my inward parts; you knitted me together in my mother's womb. . . . Your eyes saw my unformed substance; in your book were written, every one of them, the days that were formed for me, when as yet there were none of them."

First of all, I realized that God had created me to be physically the person He wanted me to be, birth defects and all. When I look at David's phrase, "you knitted me together in my mother's womb," I can think, "David, you did not know anything about genetics that we know today," but the truth is, the Holy Spirit, who guided David to write those words, knows infinitely more about genetics than the most brilliant scientists. So when He guides David to say, "You knitted me together in my mother's womb," He is saying that God so controlled the genetics that I became physically exactly the person He wanted me to be. The same is true about the fact that the days that were ordained for me, including those early difficult days, were written in His book before one of them came to be.

So I was born physically exactly the way God wanted me to be and to parents who were poor, uneducated, and socially isolated, all because that was the plan God ordained for me before I was born.

But if you fast-forward my life to the present, you have to be amazed at what God has done for a cross-eyed, partially deaf boy growing up in poverty alongside the railroad tracks. As I think of myself, I am continually reminded of the words of Psalm 40:1-3:

> *I waited patiently for the LORD; he inclined to me and heard my cry. He drew me up from the pit of destruction, out of the miry bog, and set my feet upon a rock, making my steps secure. He put a new song in my mouth, a song of praise to our God. Many will see and fear, and put their trust in the LORD.*

Though David's reference to the "pit of destruction" and the "miry bog" overstates my situation, the idea of God drawing me up and setting my feet upon a rock is exactly how I view God's work in my life.

Furthermore, all that God has done, He has done solely by His grace. Apart from Christ I deserve nothing but His eternal judgment. In fact I could easily appropriate the title of one of John Bunyan's works, *Grace Abounding to the Chief of Sinners*. And I readily identify with Jacob, who was himself an amazing illustration of God's grace, when he said, "I am not worthy of the least of all the deeds of steadfast love and all the faithfulness that you have shown to your servant, for with only my staff I crossed this Jordan, and now I have become two camps" (Genesis 32:10).